Rick Cua's new book, *What Are You Known For?* is filled with God's word, interesting stories, and fresh thoughts. Every chapter is designed to motivate you as you build your life's legacy day by day and brick by brick.

Dr. Kevin Leman
New York Times Best-selling Author of *Have a New Kid by Friday* and *The Birth Order Book*

Throughout most of my long career in the music business, both as a musician and as a record executive, I have known Rick Cua. He is the essence of an authentic and generous spirit. It was an absolute honor to tour and play music with him as well as work with him in his various roles within the music industry. He has always demonstrated a genuine faith in Christ as well as an uncompromising commitment to his family and friends. I'm honored to have a friend of this caliber in my life. He has taught me and many others so much about practical faith, seeking God and walking humbly in our faith journey. His insights into scripture and the real life applications he reveals are relatable and highly motivating. I'm thrilled to see his heart conveyed so effectively through this amazing book!

Peter York
Chairman / CEO, Capitol Christian Music Group

In a world where so many people approach life in a *transactional* way, I've long admired Rick Cua's *relational* approach. I always got the sense that here was a man who cared passionately about music, but even more deeply about people. That heart comes across so strongly in this lovely, conversational book—*What Are You Known For?*—and as you read it you'll catch much wisdom about life, love, faith and purpose. Enjoy!

Matt Redman
Songwriter / Worship Musician

My good friend Rick Cua lives life to the fullest! He is curious about everyone and everything, and he cares deeply about it all. This book is like having a cup of coffee with a fascinating, joyful and generous friend. No long lectures … just creative insights into amazing everyday things mixed with eternal truths. It inspired me to ponder, to smile and to grow. Enjoy!

Dr. Wess Stafford
President Emeritus, Compassion International
Author of *Too Small to Ignore* and *Just a Minute*

Rick's music has had and continues to have a huge influence on my life; both in my younger teenage years and also as I have continued on my journey growing as a Christian. Today Rick has taken some of those same life lessons he sung about over the years and placed them into great, concise words of wisdom, which are easy to understand and apply to our lives. I would recommend this book to help any Christian grow in their walk with God. Another great job by Rick Cua!

Jay DePalmo
CEO, Mardel Christian and Education Stores

As Pastor and friend I have watched Rick Cua live his life loving God and loving others. His simple mission has always inspired and lifted the people around him. You will find that same inspiration in the pages of *What Are You Known For?* Want to think, feel and ultimately be better, for Jesus and all those you love? I highly recommend you pick up a copy of this humble yet powerful little book...and share it with others!

Steve Berger
Pastor, Grace Chapel, Franklin, TN

What Are You Known For? is an incredible book with great content. It is fast paced and easy to read. With short chapters, FULL of scripture, you can read several a day or make it a daily devotional. Rick Cua is a brilliant man with so much wisdom from following Jesus' example in listening to others. Each chapter of this book is filled with plenty of encouragement to get you through the day. I can say from firsthand experience that Rick is one of the very best communicators I've ever met. People of all ages love to hear this man teach!

Joe White
President, Kanakuk Kamps

I have appreciated Rick Cua's various skill sets now for over 30 years. As a musician, songwriter, record company executive, partner in producing the Christian Musician Summit Conferences in Buffalo, NY for 8 years, a long time writer for my Christian Musician magazine, a mentor/advisor to me and even better than all those things—I have known Rick as a Godly friend who always makes me want to be a better person when I am around him. If you asked me for a great example in my life of a man I know who walks with real down-to-earth rubber-meets-the-road Christian integrity...Rick Cua is at the #1 spot on a very short list. All that said—I would gladly read anything Rick Cua deems worthy of writing.

Bruce Adolph
Publisher

Rick Cua has more to offer than music. Even though he's an all-time great in the music industry, he is known more for who he is than just what he has done or what gifts he has. With the turn of each page, I know every reader of this book will be the beneficiary of the same wisdom and love many of us have experienced from Rick for so many years.

Dr. Jerry Gillis
Lead Pastor, The Chapel, Buffalo, NY

When Rick Cua is telling stories, I want to listen. In the messy effort of trying to combine business, art and faith, Rick's life has shone like a beacon in the night to all of us in the Christian music community. This book tells the tales that only Rick can tell, and in a way that is completely unique to him. You'll be drawn in by his experiences and perspective, but you'll be changed by the Gospel that is living on every page.

John Mays
Sr. VP - A&R, Centricity Records

Rick Cua's "truth" erupts out of his soul, runs through his fingertips onto the fret board of a vintage Fender Precision, down a ¼-inch cable, through a bass amplifier and into the ears and hearts of his listeners. That, to me, is Rick's truth, one that is his own—that only he can preach—sound infused with Spirit. And he's laid it down loud and clear for years. Now, however, a second helping. Rick's confessions and admonitions in *What Are You Known For?* have a sweetness of spirit that strikes me as eminently trustworthy. And, like his musical gift, it hits the heart as true.

Dave Perkins, M.Div., Ph.D., Associate Director:
Religion in the Arts and Contemporary Culture
The Divinity School of Vanderbilt University, Nashville, TN

In life, one often wonders about their legacy. As we age we ask ourselves, who are we, what have we experienced, and how can we give back? Knowing Rick Cua for over twenty-five years, I have seen first hand, a man who has lived his life loving and serving others by using the gifts God has blessed him with. Now, we all get to share a glimpse of his journey through *What Are You Known For?* A ministry partner for decades, I have witnessed Rick's compassion and thoughtfulness up close. He has blessed hundreds of thousands through his music, his love for Christ and his passion for the brokenhearted.

Stephen Tybor III
CEO / Founder, Eight Days Of Hope

Anything that comes from the heart, mind and pen of Rick Cua is sure to be full of truth and wonder, in equal measures. A long time musician and "longer time" passionate follower of Christ, Rick reminds us that being known for a life that looks like Christ is the fullest measure of a life well-lived. Do yourself a favor and drink from the "wisdom well" that is Rick Cua.

Allison Allen
Speaker and Author of *Shine* and *Thirsty for More*

The principles found in *What Are You Known For?* are reinforced by Scriptures, stories and Holy Spirit wisdom from a man who has lived his life for Christ. My friend of many years, Rick Cua, shares truth in a way that's often entertaining and always insightful. I would encourage you to visit these pages and add them to your play-book for a life well lived.

Nancy Alcorn
Founder & President, Mercy Multiplied

I loved reading Rick's new book for multiple reasons, but mainly two: 1) It reminds me of how much I love this man and how great a positive influence he has been in my life. His wisdoms permeate my being and push me closer to God & fellow man in ways I don't always notice til I do something like read this book, and I am reminded "Yep, got that one from Ricky!" And 2) I'm really thrilled to know that the rest of the world has the opportunity to hear from Rick still/again. His folksy and Scriptural how-to's are gold waiting to be cashed in by any of us. Time spent with Rick—in person or on these pages—is never time wasted.

Bob Halligan Jr
Songwriter / 30 million units sold, Leader of Ceili Rain

I've been gleaning wisdom from Rick Cua for nearly half of my life; he lives, speaks, and gives it daily just by being who he is. He inspires me to be known above all else as a Godly man. As you read *What Are You Known For?* you will be encouraged through every story and situation he recalls from his amazing life. God is truly at the center of his being.

Tom Lane
Worship Leader, Songwriter / President, The Bridge -
A Joseph Company

My dear friend Rick Cua has come up with a beautifully written book on what it is to be human. His stories and essays are full of practical, wonderful insights on living a life that will leave a legacy. Pick up *What Are You Known For?*, and do what's in the book. And you'll soon find out what you'll be known for!

Joe Battaglia, President, Renaissance Communications,
Broadcaster & Author of *Unfriended: Finding True
Community in a Disconnected Culture*

I've always believed in destiny; the sovereign purpose for which we've been created. Fulfilling our destiny brings God glory, gives us great joy, and ultimately advances His Kingdom. As we discover and live out our destiny, "what we will be known for" is also being shaped and formed. Legacy lessons cannot be taught by the young entrepreneur who's never "been there." Rick Cua is not old, but he has lived a unique and special life that has given him stories and insights that we can all learn from. I love this book, the lessons he shares, and the way he shares them. I will buy this book for my grown children and for the many leaders, both young and old, that I get to do life with.

Rev. Scott Olson
President & CEO, One Collective

I highly recommend Rick Cua's new book *What You Are Known For?* Rick has found a way to connect with the seasons of our lives and the things we encounter to help us see God's handiwork in it all. As you read through each chapter you will think, laugh and be challenged but most of all it will touch your heart. I saw myself, my ups and downs, in the pages of this book. I was encouraged in my faith while challenged in my heart to continue to grow and seek to make a difference in the world around me. God's wisdom is practically revealed in these pages. Make this the one book you read this year.

Ron Jutze
Director of Operations, The Word For You Today

In our congregation, there are few people more beloved than our dear Pastor Rick Cua. It's because he has touched every life he has encountered with gentle grace and deep wisdom. With years of experience ministering to people of all walks of life and in various situations, he has gathered wisdom along the way that honors God's Truth every time. We are blessed that he has taken the time to write these truths down for us in *What Are You Known For?*

Janice Gaines
Recording Artist, Motown Gospel

Rick Cua is the most "half-full" kind of friend you will ever want in your life. Spending time with him in the pages of this book will allow you to see God enter the "everyday" situations and decisions we all face in our lifetime.

Donna M. Russo
Festival Director / CFO, Kingdom Bound Ministries

Rick Cua has demonstrated a life of devotion to ministry and his family. With a successful career in music, Rick is an example of how to respectfully and gracefully engage in society as a Christian. This book is filled with enriching stories, uplifting wisdom and practical life tips. It is a must-read for Christians who seek practical inspiration for their daily walk.

Tore Stautland
Media Executive; CEO, TMG Studios;
NRB, President's Council

One of the greatest gifts a man can give is the wealth of wisdom he has accumulated over his rich life. With his new book, Rick Cua humbly offers these practical, but deep morsels of wisdom, like breadcrumbs guiding us in all ways to our Savior.

EJ Gaines
Co-Executive Director, Motown Gospel /
Vice President of Marketing, Capitol Christian Music Group

Intriguing, joy-filled, practical, inspiring, deeply encouraging and filled with surprises. These captivating stories, told out of a very creative walk-with-God, by one of the most integrated Christians I know, Rick Cua, bring great inspiration and very practical help to anyone who wants to know God better, and live out a life that pleases Him. Rick draws from walking with Jesus over many years—from musician, to rock star, to executive, to pastor—to give very strategic encouragement that will help anyone better touch God, receive from God, and grow deeper in God. This is a must read!!

Rev. Dr. Byron Spradlin
President, Artists in Christian Testimony Intl, Franklin, TN

What does someone with over five decades of performing, worshipping, ministering, and serving others do with all of the wisdom and experiences he has collected through the years? He shares it with the rest of us! Rick Cua has modeled for all of us a life well lived. He is a man who has been singularly devoted to his faith, purposed in his desire to love others, and driven to make a difference in this world. This book is deep and rich with life stories that will make you laugh, make you think, and make you more certain of the answer to his question, *What Are You Known For?*

Lisa Murray
LMFT & Author of *Peace for a Lifetime*

Rick Cua has wonderfully woven together personal memories and experiences that have impacted his very life, career and calling. His ability to capture those experiences and communicate them in a clear and compelling way is to be highly commended. The Life lessons that he shares are candid, caring and compassionate as he aligns them with the powerful truths of the Word of God which have shaped his life and destiny. The title of this book, *What Are You Known For?*, can be understood as an important question that should motivate all of us to take sometime to do a spiritual life inventory. If we will make our life decisions based on the answer to this question and its impact on the Legacy we leave behind, I believe we will not be disappointed when our time has come to exit into eternity. Thank you Rick for this wonderful work of love: It will truly be a blessing to every reader regardless of where they are coming from and where they are at in their individual lives.

Rev. Giulio Lorefice Gabeli
Senior Pastor, Westwood Community Church / Canadian Liason for the Knesset Christian Allies Caucus (KCAC), Israel Allies Foudation

Rick Cua exemplifies the compassion of Christ in his every action as a leader in our church and community. His experience, strength and hope pervade every word of this engaging book. Rick's Italian roots, success in the music industry and current position as a Pastoral Care pastor offer a humorous, creative and spiritual history to drawn upon. His insights take real life and transform them into Biblical teaching moments that will bless Christians of all ages.

Amanda Cecconi
CEO and Founder, Punching Nun Group

There are some people in your life whose positive impact is felt strongly in their presence and lingers persistently in their absence. Pastor Rick Cua is one of those people for me. My heart leapt when I first heard that he had taken the time to write down a few of his life experiences, filtered through the lens of his love for Jesus and His obvious influence in Rick's life. With *What Are You Known For?*, Rick has blessed us all a timeless gift of legacy from a man whose persistent encouragement into my own life has helped me understand the way God thinks of me, despite my obvious flaws and imperfections. It is a gift we can all cherish and pass along to the next generation.

Bob Thompson
Managing Partner, RiverTree Consulting
Past President and Executive Director - Christian
Festival Assocation

I loved looking at life and its lessons through the filter and lens of Rick Cua's heart. I don't know many people longer that I do Rick, and I have watched his glorious journey thru life thru most of mine. He's seen it all and has grown to place I believe we all wish to find. Take the time to start thinking about it while trying to discover what you yourself...are known for, through these inspiring short stories.

Victor Sansone, President, Big Night Out Events
ABC / Disney Radio, 33 Years Operating President & GM
BOD & Former Chairman of CMA

For anyone who wants to leave a legacy but isn't sure how, *What Are You Known For?* offers a gentle reminder of how the little choices we make each day can make a difference that lasts beyond our lifetime. With wisdom, grit and a little humor along the way, Rick's earnest reflections will inspire you to celebrate the small stuff as you lean into the big picture God has planned for your life!

Constance Rhodes, Founder and CEO, FINDINGbalance; Author, *The Art of Being: Reflections on the Beauty and the Risk of Embracing Who We Are*

Rick Cua has heart and you can feel it beating as you hold his book in your hands. I've known Rick for over 30 years but more than that I have witnessed his life through the scope of his personal commitment to others. He lives what he breathes—God's Holy Spirit—as he takes timeless wisdom and portrays that in his daily walk.

The stories in this book are earthy, gut level real, poignant, inspiring and sometimes downright fascinating in their portrayal of how wonderfully interesting people can be when you observe them with an open heart. Rick says this about his late Father… "My Father, Buzzy, was a man who devoted his life to his family and loved everyone he met. It didn't matter if he had two minutes with you. After those two minutes you walked away feeling better about yourself." After reading *What Are You Known For?* You too will feel like you spent time with our Heavenly Father and you will surely walk away feeling better about yourself!

Ken Mansfield
Author & Former US Manager Apple Records
www.mainmansfield.com

I read a lot of self-help books, devotionals, nonfiction and fiction. All I can say is that I fought between wanting to read the next chapter with basking in the space of the existing chapter I was on. This material is light, easy to read, conversational yet deep and meaningful. It strikes just the right chord to get you thinking...and yet doesn't take you to a place that causes you to overthink, get bogged down or tired. I felt somehow more relaxed, more fresh, more aware.

Renée Rizzo
President & CEO, Hope Clinic For Women

WHAT ARE YOU KNOWN FOR?

BUILDING YOUR LEGACY ONE BRICK AT A TIME

RICK CUA

AFTK

ALL FOR THE KING MEDIA

ISBN: 978-0-578-65821-6 (Print)
ISBN: 978-0-578-65822-3 (eBook)

Printed in the United States of America

DEDICATION

*To My Wife, no one has helped shape me
to be more like Christ than you.*

In these 50 years you have walked with me
on the high road, and early on, persevered with me
on the low road. We have used every experience
to strengthen our marriage and to help strengthen others
along the way. (Romans 8:28) Your love, courage,
perseverance and wisdom have been a gift that I am
eternally grateful for. You are my love, my coach,
partner, best friend and so much more.

*I love you Diana Cua.
Here's to You. Here's to Us.*

CONTENTS

INTRODUCTION

The Bible's two greatest commandments, Love God and Love Others, have resonated with me for decades. Keeping this in focus has been a personal mission and a daily goal. This and other strong biblical truths are foundational life scriptures that occur more than once within the pages of *What Are You Known For?* God's truth within these Scriptures have greatly influenced my life as a Christian and continue to motivate me to live my life according to the words of Christ. We all make mistakes and have had moments of bad judgment but let's not let that overshadow a life filled with confession, repentance and following Jesus.

The sum of what we have done on this earth follows us to heaven. But at the same time it's also left behind as our legacy. That legacy starts at birth and locks into history when we take our last breath. If you are reading this you still have the great benefit of making sure your legacy contains elements worthy of leaving behind for those you love and our world at large. Something that's helped me greatly is the example given in God's Word describing the fruit of the spirit. Reading that passage often and making sure I am representing these truths well helps align me for the day ahead.

What Are You Known For? is filled with stories and scriptures that have helped define my life. Just a slice of it not yet the whole. By God's Grace there's more good stuff to share ahead and more missteps too but less of them I trust with each passing year.

We are building our legacy one brick at a time. Every brick part of a solid foundation that becomes your life story. A story to encourage others for decades to come.

I hope this book will help you live with one eye on the now and the other one on the future so that when we pause to examine our lives we will see Jesus in all of it.

"What is it that makes this or that person remarkable in a way that exemplifies God, not just in a single act or accomplishment, but for a lifetime?"

Identity

WHAT ARE YOU KNOWN FOR?

I was recalling a story, not long ago, that got me thinking about what we will be known for through and beyond our lives. Will it be our work ethic, how well we communicated with people, the way we loved our families and others, what special dish we cooked or something totally bizarre?

The Glass Eater

Somewhere in the early seventies, our band found ourselves regularly playing at a club in Utica, New York called The Little Big Man, probably named after the 1970 Dustin Hoffman film. It was a very cool room, long and narrow with a big, high stage at one end. Everything was painted flat black, which was good for the black-lights that were very popular at the time. The place was always filled with colorful characters and strong smells of patchouli, which I still enjoy to this day. There at the club, I remember the first time I saw him. A tall, thin and willowy guy. He would dance by himself in the middle of the dance floor while sipping his drink as we played something from Cream, Mott The Hoople or David Bowie. He would just move to the music in a very slow and overly dramatic way. That was odd enough in and of itself, but the real showstopper was after he finished his drink, he ate the glass! True story! Bite by bite he chewed, crunched and swallowed the glass that minutes before held his favorite libation. Boy, that was weird. And we were all mesmerized.

He Made Us Laugh, Feel Loved and Important

Then there was Freddy Crittela. Freddy was a childhood friend who loved music and loved the food by which he made his living. We would go to Crittela's Italian Restaurant, and Freddy would always come out from the kitchen in his white T-shirt covered with sauce stains—his medals, we called them. He would pull up a chair and sit at our table, telling us stories. He made us laugh, feel loved and important and filled our bellies with some of the best Italian food we would ever eat, short of our own kitchens, of course. Freddy's in heaven now. Maybe the glass eater, too. But I think of Freddy way more.

And there was my Father, Buzzy. Ninety years old when he went to be with Jesus. Remembered by all as a man who devoted his life to his family and loved everyone he met. It didn't matter if he only had two minutes with you. After those two minutes, you walked away feeling better about yourself.

Kindness Is Hard to Forget

Dad had a small spiral notebook he kept in his breast pocket, and he always had his camera with him. He would take pictures of strangers all the time and then get their name and address so he could send them a print. I can't tell you how often people would tell us about Dad's kindness and the photo they unexpectedly received from him. He was a great guitar player, too, and the reason I play music.

I could go on and on about so many. My wonderful wife, my kids, my grandkids, my siblings and some of you who are reading this, I'm sure. But the point of all this isn't to keep going on about someone else. It's to point us in a direction that will make us remarkable for years to come.

A Good Measure of a Man or Woman

God's Word tells us in Matthew 7:16 that "You will know them by their fruits." What are those fruits?

3

Galatians 5:22,23 says "But the fruit of the Spirit is love, joy, peace, patience, kindness, goodness, faithfulness, gentleness, and self-control" (ESV). I look at this as a kind of personal mission statement, one we can continually look back at to see if our lives and actions line up.

In John 13:35, we are told also that men will know we are disciples of Jesus by our love for one another. Loving God and loving others can only lead to a legacy that will be something for others to celebrate. If a life started and stopped with "He can really play that bass" or "What a great cook" or "She has so many degrees," you might ask yourself...what else? Those things are all good. But what is it that makes this or that person remarkable in a way that exemplifies God, not just in a single act or accomplishment, but for a lifetime?

What is it about someone that most makes you want to be like him or her? Hopefully more than one thing. For all I know, the glass eater might have been the kindest man in his neighborhood or a missionary for Christ, but all I saw was the circus act. Very entertaining for sure, but not something you would want to imitate.

Charles Caleb Colton coined the phrase, "Imitation is the best form of flattery." When you admire someone, you imitate them. Let's live our lives for Christ, working always to be more like Him. Let His virtues shine through our lives like lifesaving beacons to a world looking for leaders to emulate.

This chapter started with a question that's really a big deal. And it ends with one, too. One that can only be answered by your actions and the witness of others: What are YOU known for?

"People are moved to change,

or motivated to move upward,

by everything you do that reflects

God's heart for people

and His purpose for you."

Service

TWO

DO GOOD AND DON'T COME DOWN

*"Do all the good you can. By all the means you can.
In all the ways you can. In all the places you can.
At all the times you can. To all the people you can.
As long as ever you can."*
— John Wesley (Anglican cleric and Christian theologian)

Our salvation isn't based on works (Ephesians 2:8-10). Yet, we also know that faith without works is dead (James 2:17). Nothing functions in a more perfect way than the double blessing of doing good: You bless others and you get blessed in the process (Luke 6:38). While getting a blessing isn't our motive for helping others or doing good works, it sure is a nice byproduct, especially since the double blessing is by God's design. You reap what you sow...what goes around comes around (2 Corinthians 9:6). It's a law understood by most.

Some people get locked up in their thinking because they believe doing good only comes in big packages containing big ideas. Truth is, the simple things of life—like being kind, concerning yourself with others and spreading God's love in word and deed—qualify at the same level. Good is good no matter how lofty the plan or how regular the deed. God loves it all. Plus, people are moved to change, or motivated to move upward, by everything you do that reflects God's heart for people and His purpose for you.

Recognize Distractions and Don't Comply

The caution is that for every step we make toward the continuation of a good work, our enemy, Satan, makes a step to block us. Usually it's with some temptation or distraction that might not in itself be evil but will slow us down or even derail us from the good work God is calling us to do. When Nehemiah was rebuilding the wall in Jerusalem, the enemy king sent soldiers to distract him as the work was nearing completion. Nehemiah's response to the soldiers' requests for him to come away from the work encourages me to this day. Nehemiah recognized the potential distraction and refused to comply.

"So I sent messengers to them, saying, 'I am doing a great work, so that I cannot come down. Why should the work cease while I leave it and go down to you?'" (Nehemiah 6:3)

What's your distraction? What pulls you off course and disengages you from completing the good work in front of you that will bless God, a certain person or the many in your path, and yourself as well? What is that tempting smell of honey that rises as a threat from the ground up to the top of the ladder where your good work nears completion?

Ask the Lord to help you know when a distraction comes your way and what it looks like, whether obviously evil or appearing to be good. Ask Him to help you realize the importance of the work He has for you. Pray that the Holy Spirit's discernment would allow you to quickly identify things that will take you down from the good work that He is doing in and through you. And when that thing confronts you, speak out loud and with authority to the Evil One who sent it and say as Nehemiah did, "I'm doing a great work and I cannot come down!"

"We are made to appreciate beauty,

and we do that best

when we are free and whole."

THREE

BEAUTY IN THE DANCE

Following Christ is a dance with many moves. A few steps to the right, a few to the left, forward, back, the occasional spin, dip and a lot of grace. We can look at it as the dance of life. There's no exact formula on how to move, but God's Word and the voice of the Holy Spirit become the music we move to. The words, rhythm, passion, pause and discernment guide our steps. Every one of us is different. Each day, every situation, our encounters with others, and even our thought processes, become our own unique combination of patterns. Sometimes you move quickly with confidence, sometimes slowly with thoughtful discernment. No matter the tempo, to dance you must move.

I remember being at a well-known ballroom in Tampa, Florida one night to see an old friend play drums with his trio. They were a pretty great band, but what really captured me was the ballroom dancers dressed to the nines out on the floor in their tuxedos and long dresses. Hair slicked and pulled back with textbook posture and an air of confidence that you couldn't help but admire. I was drawn in by their grace, moved by their skill and brought to tears by the sheer beauty of it.

Then, more recently, I saw a video on YouTube of an older, portly man dancing to music in a strange and awkward way. Joy was in his heart and on his face as he glided weirdly across my screen. Oddly, I had the same reaction watching him as I did with the highly-skilled dancers in Tampa.

True Beauty and Joy Comes from the Lord

So, what was it that touched me so deeply? The only commonality was the fact that in both instances people were dancing. As I thought about this more, I realized there was something else happening: people doing something honest and harmless that made them feel good. Expressing joy in their own way with total freedom and confidence. The sophisticated dancers weren't fazed by all the eyes that were upon them. And my unusual friend didn't care that he was being filmed for thousands to watch. They were all, in their own way, in their own world. I'm not sure of the spiritual condition of any of them, but I do know that what they felt was God-given. And it was the beauty and joy of the Lord I experienced as I watched them all move. It reminded me of Proverbs 23:7, which says "For as he thinks in his heart, so is he."

With the dancers in Tampa, there was something driving them way more than the precise movements they learned and executed perfectly; it was the beauty of what they felt when they were out there doing it. It's the same with our not-so-precise YouTuber who just had to move when he felt the joy rising up in his being. When his heart spoke to his feet, he expressed his happiness in his own unique way.

There are times when our move from feeling blah to feeling joyful is a short jump. And then there are occasions when we are in deep grief, and the words of Psalm 30:11a, "You have turned for me my mourning into dancing," comes as great relief.

We all dance one way or another, and there are also times we're bystanders or onlookers. Some of the watchers don't look for very long because their own pain prevents them from being moved by the happiness in others. We are made to appreciate beauty, and we do that best when we are free and whole. We need to remember that beauty becomes harder to recognize when we are in pain.

Don't Miss the Moment

I was barely 13 at a Lincoln Jr. High School dance where the girls spent the evening dancing and us boys spent the evening watching. The dance was scheduled to end at 10:30 pm, and I'm sure the teachers and chaperones were more than ready to call it a night. My friend, Moey Hale, was running the Jukebox, and at 10:25, he decided to put on a slow song to close out the event. I'm not sure how it happened, but every adolescent male finally made his way to the center of the gym floor and, almost trance-like, walked up to a female student and said something like, "wanna dance?" It was more involuntary instinct than good sense, but it was the moment all of us turned a corner.

We almost missed it, but those glorious five minutes on Vine Street changed everything. Better late than never, we seized an innocent moment of joy and learned a valuable life lesson: don't wait until something good is almost over to jump in; make every minute count. I'm pretty sure a tear didn't fall that night like it did in Tampa, but I do know that all of my being—body, soul and spirit—was fully engaged.

So my question is, will we make the absolute most of our lives by embracing the joy that God has put before us? Will we move quickly towards opportunity? Will we recognize beauty in whatever package it comes in? Will we take long, lingering looks to see what God may be saying? Will we get out of our chair and let our fellow dancers circle us while we passionately share the joy and beauty we've been given? Will we follow Him for life and love and healing? But most importantly, will we show our world His beauty in the dance?

"When we make the effort to enter into someone's life and take a genuine interest in the things that interest them, trust is established and we become safe. Perhaps even safe enough to have access to their heart for the sake of the Gospel."

Relevance

GOD WEARS A HOODIE

Some of the greatest joys in life come from our grand-kids. Those sweet little voices that call us Nonna and Poppy, Gramma and Grampa, Memaw and Pepaw or whatever your term of endearment is. In some ways they're our kids all over again and in some ways they are one of a kind. And the things they say...some things that make us belly laugh! And some things that speak a truth way beyond their years, making us ponder their thoughts like philosophers hot on the trail of the meaning of life.

One evening at dinner, our grandchildren, Luke and Eva, were eating their daddy's smoked ribs like it was their last meal. At ages seven and four, no vegan menu for them. Somehow during the dinner conversation, the topic of Adam and Eve came up, so our daughter Nina began to unpack the story. When she got to the part about Eve eating the apple, she explained to Luke that Adam and Eve for the first time realized they were naked. "Naked!" said Luke...."How about God, was He naked too?" We all froze for a moment thinking about the question when Luke said, "No, no, no, He wasn't naked, God wears a hoodie!" Obviously, he was referring to Jesus because we all know it's Jesus who wears the hoodie. We gave it to him though since Jesus is, in fact, God.

Be in Life and Make a Difference

I spent days thinking about Luke's comment, knowing that there was something deeper to discover other than the laughter we all enjoyed at dinner that night. The word that kept coming back to me was relevance, something we should all strive for. Being connected to the world around us, being involved in life, making a difference; having a voice because people will relate to us when they know we relate to them.

And who's more relevant than God? He's everything! The Alpha and Omega, the beginning and the end. All of life comes from Him. He's the author, the Designer, He's time, He's timeless. He has nothing to prove—He's God after all! He is sovereign over history, and history exists because of Him. God meets each of us exactly where we are. He cares about what we care about. We don't need to put on a special suit to meet with Him. We just need to bring ourselves and open our hearts to the one who made us.

The thing to focus on here is OUR relevance to others. Everyone should wear a hoodie, at least figuratively. It's that kind of mindset that will make us want to connect with others; make us want to be viewed and understood as those who are truly interested in the people and world around us. How can we have influence if we aren't interested or really caring to join in, engage, grow, keep up?

Relate to Others and Learn New Things

When I'm in a conversation with someone, usually in the fifty-plus range, sometimes I'll hear them say things like, "I don't use a computer, don't want a tablet and certainly don't need a smart phone...I'm just not interested." The first thing I say is, go out and get all three! Figure it out and engage yourself with the things this culture engages in. Relate to others, learn new things, stretch yourself—don't check out. In a manner of speaking, it's like fitness: you won't have to fight to lose the belly if you don't get one in the first place. This is not judgement. It's experience! Be the best that you can be no matter where you are in life. Usually the folks that say those things to me have a whole list of people and things they are disappointed with. They don't want to grow, yet they are hurt, living a life masked by contempt, feeling that the world has passed them by.

We are an interesting bunch. In 1 Corinthians 9:22 the Apostle Paul says that he became all things to all men so as to save a few. He did this by being there, being relevant in the situation. In Acts 10:34, we are reminded that God is no respecter of persons, He doesn't show partiality, He loves us and is actually interested in the things we are interested in. So, how will others relate to us and Christ in us if we live in a cave? Show up from time to time. Put on the hoodie, jump in the water, join the party, keep your values and share them. Your only common ground may be your smart phone or tablet, but relevance needs to start somewhere and usually leads to relationship. What did Jesus have in common with the woman at the well? Probably nothing other than thirst, but the impact He had on her by showing up was life-changing and a lesson that has never stopped being taught.

This is what it means to be relevant: to be closely connected or appropriate to the matter at hand. That can apply to anything. But what greater matter at hand is there than people? That's really it, isn't it? Relevance for the purpose of connecting with people relationally and seeing how that relationship can be a blessing. Walking through that eventual open door that comes in a growing relationship gives access to you and the message of love you are carrying. And how great is the risk? It's nothing at all compared to the lost opportunity of seeing someone say yes to the greatest gift of all. When we make the effort to enter into someone's life and take a genuine interest in the things that interest them, trust is established and we become safe. Perhaps even safe enough to have access to their heart for the sake of the Gospel.

Does God wear a hoodie? Like no one else! And there's one in your size and favorite color hanging in your closet waiting for you. You only have to put it on once because when you do, you'll realize the God-ordained joy of connecting with others by clothing yourself with the lifegiving message of Jesus Christ and sharing it through a life that's fully engaged!

"Let's let God shine His light

on every area of our lives

leaving no unrighteous space in the dark."

Righteousness

LIGHT BLACK

I remember well the early days of my faith, when I was shedding my bad habits like a snake sheds old skin. I began walking away from things that ran contrary to the Word of God. One by one I said goodbye to the obvious stuff. Then, as I was convicted, each subsequent tier of bad behavior was purposely driven out of my life. There were, however, a few things that I wanted to hang onto. They may have been mostly inactive, but they were still there. Looking back, it was like burying the hatchet with the end of the handle poking out of the dirt just enough to grip and pull out, re-activating that thing you thought you finally left behind. It's also like a faucet that's almost off. Just a drip every so often until you mess up again. That occasional drip returns to a steady flow. How much better off I would have been just leaving ALL the junk behind. Not a little here and there but all of it all at once. A ceremonial cleansing with no hesitation or regret.

Many times, the enemy of our good behavior is believing the lie that when you engage in your remaining guilty pleasures, you will somehow fit in and be happy. Acting on that will never move you forward, bring lasting joy or allow you to fulfill the destiny that God has placed before you. Your momentary pleasure instantly becomes a handicap that if left unchecked can become terminal.

1 John 1:7 says "But if we walk in the light as He is in the light, we have fellowship with one another, and the blood of Jesus Christ His Son cleanses us from all sin." If we walk in God's light there are no shadows, no darkness at all, we are cleansed.

Stay the Course and Don't Look Back

The issue here is: Are we really committed? To be clear, commitment doesn't mean perfection. It means that you have made up your mind to stay the course and not look back. You will have a misstep here and there, but it won't deflate you IF you quickly pick yourself up, repent and move forward. You will feel bad and have some level of disappointment, as you should, but it's not derailment.

It's interesting to me that reality tells us we WILL mess up, but our determination not to fail shouldn't allow us to consider doing something that we will regret. Honestly the battle is really in our mind. It takes just as long to make the right decision as it does the wrong decision. What happens is we believe the lie by dwelling on it instead of taking that thought captive and getting rid of it.

Many times, we consider the really bad stuff the really big stuff. That's just not the case. If it doesn't reflect God's Word, it's all really big. The enemy will continually tell us...that's just a small thing, but the Holy Spirit will convict us of our righteousness every time...if we are listening.

John 16:8-11 Tells us "And when He (The Holy Spirit) has come, He will convict the world of sin, and of righteousness, and of judgment: of sin, because they do not believe in Me; of righteousness, because I go to My Father and you see Me no more; of judgement because the ruler of this world is judged."

I always thought that the Holy Spirit convicts us of our sin but nowhere in the New Testament do we see this. The Holy Spirit convicts the world of their sin and us of our righteousness. In other words, when we sin, we convict ourselves. This conviction comes because The Holy Spirit reminds us that we are righteous. So, if we are living in an unrighteous way, a friend, not witnessing our bad behavior may tell us that he admires how wonderfully we are living. Immediately our sin is called to mind, again because the Holy Spirit convicts us of our righteousness which helps us quickly identify our sin and we hopefully repent.

Lasting Victory Comes When We Do Our Part

We're not alone. In 1 Corinthians 10:13 we read "No temptation has overtaken you except such as is common to man; but God is faithful, who will not allow you to be tempted beyond what you are able, but with the temptation will also make the way of escape, that you may be able to bear it." Again, it's up to us, we have a part to play. God always does His part and we must do ours if we want lasting victory.

Let's let God shine His light on every area of our lives leaving no unrighteous space in the dark. Remember this truth from 1 Corinthians 5:6-7 "Your glorying is not good. Do you not know that a little leaven leavens the whole lump? Therefore, purge out the old leaven, that you may be a new lump, since you truly are unleavened. For indeed Christ, our Passover, was sacrificed for us."

We are living in a world where the black gets blacker and the white gets whiter. We all need to choose who we will serve and like it or not our choice becomes evident by our actions. In the words of the great Wilson Pickett, "Ninety-nine and a half just won't due" and neither will light black. You're either living right or you're not. Paul encourages us in Romans 13:14 to..."put on the Lord

Jesus Christ, and make no provision for the flesh, to fulfill its lusts."

We can do it...God says we can! Walk in the light...lose the leaven...take every thought captive, flood your light black with His marvelous light and never forget God's promise; "For I the LORD your God, will hold your right hand, saying to you, 'Fear not, I will help you.'" Isaiah 41:13

"We are the recipients of years of wisdom, successful methodology perfected by trial and error, and all of it from the love of others."

Teaching

THE DOUBLE KNOT

It's funny how old memories, after many decades, can just pop up now and then and say hello. For as long as I can remember, every time I tie my shoes, I tie a double knot. As I'm doing it I sometimes think to myself, "good, they won't come untied and I won't trip." I never gave it much thought until recently when I remembered my mom teaching me how to do that and why I should. Teaching others takes time and purpose. If you're like most you may wonder if your effort is doing any good. I would say that it is, but even if your tutelage goes unheeded, do it anyway.

The exact moment a lesson is being learned is sometimes never recalled, but the result of that thoughtful exchange may last a lifetime and is often passed down to others. Some of the things you do are instinct, but most are learned behaviors. We are the recipients of years of wisdom, successful methodology perfected by trial and error, and all of it from the love of others. "Don't do that, you might get hurt; be careful or you'll poke your eye out; bend your legs when you lift; don't run, take your time; hurry up or you'll be late; think next time". Yikes! Sometimes it feels like a litany of commands. But everyone salutes a happy ending.

If You Want Your Words to Stick Wrap Them in Kindness

Here's something to remember as you pass along value to others. Delivery is everything. If you want your words to stick, wrap them in kindness and deliver them with love. Proverbs 15:1 says that "A gentle answer turns away wrath, but a harsh word stirs up anger." (NIV) Some instruction is given without being asked, the way a parent raises a child and teaches instinctively; or, the way you mentor someone by observation and modeling. Throughout life you will also be asked a lot of questions about the everyday ways of life and faith. Regarding your answer, the level of reception and understanding from your listener will most likely be based on how you deliver your thoughts. If there is care and love in your words you will have a good listener and a good learner. 1 Peter 3:15 (NIV) emphasizes, "But in your hearts revere Christ as Lord. Always be prepared to give an answer to everyone who asks you to give the reason for the hope that you have. But do this with gentleness and respect." So why is this so important? Why can't we just live our lives, do our own thing and let others do the same? Not feel the responsibility and not have to take the risk of wondering if what we've got is valuable and worth sharing?

Depending on your student, teaching can take a lot out of you. But one reason this is so important is because it's modeled throughout the Bible and emphasized in 2 Timothy 2:1-2 "You then, my son, be strong in the grace that is in Christ Jesus. And the things you have heard me say in the presence of many witnesses entrust to reliable people who will also be qualified to teach others." (NIV) That's foundational knowledge for all of us as we go through life learning AND teaching. For most there comes a time where teaching just comes out of us...our gifts, talents and experiences make room for us in this life as God's word says in Proverbs 18:16a. This increases incrementally as we move on in years.

Recipients and Deliverers

Another reason this is such a valuable part of our journey, is because we are commanded to love one another. When we love and care about each other—the second greatest commandment—we are eager to share all kinds of wisdom. From practical life lessons to philosophy we are not only recipients of the experience of others but deliverers of the same.

To be effective teachers—and we all can be—we need to know who we are in Christ. Who He says we are. Nothing builds our confidence more than knowing how God feels about us. This is where it starts. What God says to us in so many ways is that we are loved, we are accepted and in Him we possess all that's needed to not only complete our mission on this planet, but help others complete theirs too.

There is joy of course in doing things yourself, but many times even more joy in teaching someone else how to do it, and then celebrating their success in which you truly have a part. The wish of most great teachers is that their students surpass their own accomplishments. How wonderful to know that when you merge the talent and gifting of your student with your own library of knowledge, you get someone who's ability to soar is exponentially greater than either of you on your own.

Finally, what God has filled us with is always worth sharing. It's nugget after nugget of hope, purpose and passion. It's your recipe for life, made up of everything from step by step instructions for navigating the practical, to the contemplative stuff that dreams are made of. Learn and pass it on. Grow and share your growth. Dream and let someone in. It's your life, always richer with company.

"God has a gift wrapped up with your name
on it. To be opened and enjoyed only by you.
And the best thing about it is it's not just one
gift or one moment, it's a perpetual unwrapping
of God's gifts to us."

Expectation

JUST FOR YOU

One of the great joys of being human is participating in that beautiful moment of mutual connection that a shared experience can bring. With music, for example, I always want to bring someone into my world when I'm listening to something I love, in hopes of achieving just that. But what I'm really hoping is for them to get the exact great feeling that I get when I listen to the music that moves me. Not just come close but feel it just like I do.

Truth is, every listener has many factors at play when they listen. Where they were when they first discovered that song, who they were with, what was going on in their life, etc. Now and then we have people in our lives with musical tastes and experiences that wonderfully collide with ours. That's like reliving any other great experience with a friend. But more often what moves us may not move someone else, at least in the same way.

I can remember being with several other couples all relaxing together after a great meal. We were enjoying the evening with as close to a perfect gathering of friends as you could get. We had our iPads out and took turns being DJ. Honestly there wasn't a bad song in the bunch, they were all songs that represented the best times of our lives. So now it was my turn to share and I hit play on one of my absolute favorite songs. You know, one of a handful that lit you up with lyrics and a melody that went to the very core of your being. The one that spoke loudest to everything you believed in, that made you cry happy tears and filled you with joy. The one that made you want to share it with the whole world knowing surely they too would relate, and you would have kindred spirits surrounding you smiling and nodding their affirmation at each verse and chorus.

Well, my song wasn't even a minute in and someone actually had the nerve to engage in conversation with one of the listeners totally derailing my moment of euphoric acceptance and connection. We didn't even get through the chorus! One by one this new conversation began wooing people away from my thoughtful song selection leaving me alone with my song and disappointment.

My Unreal Expectation

What had I expected? My friends to actually take on my exact life experience and thoughts related to that tune? Did I really think that every trigger of happiness would be activated by my showcased selection and create an ecstatic union of souls from downbeat to fade out? Yes, I did!

They rained on my parade, busted my groove, popped my balloon. But actually, this wasn't about them, it was about an unreal expectation that was created by me. Truly, at the end of the day, we all have things that we wish we could share with others note for note, and word for word equally a perfectly matched experience. But some moments, I've come to realize, are made just for us.

How many times while on an airplane listening to "that song" do I tap my foot, discretely bob my head to the music or wipe a tear, imagining the person across the aisle saying, "Give me some of that!" And I excitedly take the cord to their obscenely expensive HiFi headphones, plug it into my Y adaptor from Radio Shack and all at once we are one: Plugged in like the movie character Neo, and whoever, to the matrix of our greatest hits. Uh, nope.

A Perpetual Unwrapping of God's Gifts

You know what changed everything for me? The reality that there are people all over this world enjoying their favorite music, their favorite things, their favorite people. Getting filled up with joy and gratitude to be able to have these special moments that are made, just for them. The Word tells us in in Psalm 139:14 that we are "fearfully and wonderfully made;" In other words we are all unique from our DNA to our personalities. God has a gift wrapped up with your name on it. To be opened and enjoyed only by you. And the best thing about it is it's not just one gift or one moment, it's a perpetual unwrapping of God's gifts to us. Always another one, always something to make our hearts full and ultimately prepare us to pour out God's love on others, passing it along, paying it forward because it's just so very good. That's what God does. Since the beginning of time He's created a world filled with things that we were made to love. For some of us, those things may move us in a similar way. But like a snowflake, the experience never looks exactly the same: It's one of a kind, and the experience in its entirety was designed just for you.

So, push play, tear away the wrapping paper, dive heart first into all that God has created. Every experience, every moment of unspeakable joy, every gift in front of you with your name on it. You may not be able to identically share that exact feeling with others. But others simultaneously are drinking in their own joy from every gift with THEIR name on it. And, oh, when someone else is sharing a movie, book, or song with you, although you may not be on the same cloud they are on, do your best to jump into their joy, if even just for a moment.

"Figuratively speaking if you are going to die on a hill, may it be a majestic mountain that taught you new things and will beckon you back, not that familiar low berm where average is widely celebrated."

Aspiration

GOOD, BETTER, BEST!

I can remember, as a young boy, looking at a popular department store catalog and seeing ads for merchandise that offered three buying options: Good, Better and Best. The understanding was, if the quality rose, so would the price. Even at an early age I knew that I wanted the best. Why settle for something that wasn't as good as it gets? I believe it was during the time period of that realization that I first understood that everything wasn't the best, excellence wasn't guaranteed. Once there was a delineation I immediately gravitated towards excellence, wouldn't we all? Of course, there's always the question, is it really better? How much is truth and how much is simply good marketing.

In looking back at my own life it's easy to see the areas of my productivity where I finished something too soon, stopping just short of making whatever it was the best that it could be. This happened in my songwriting and other creative endeavors as well as some of my relationships. It's almost as if I said "that's all I got" when in fact and because of Jesus I had so much more. I know it was also the lure of what was next on the agenda; that thing that I was ready to get busy on. I was like a horse at the gate, ready to get going, no longer concerned with what I was leaving behind or the fact that what I had been working on wasn't yet fully finished.

Reach Higher and Give God Your Best

Because of our human nature we quickly learn how to settle instead of reaching for the best. We often wind up with less not realizing that in our haste we may have left something unfinished that could have been great. If we had only put more time into it and treated it as something worthy of all we had our end result would have been our absolute best. This is true in every area of our lives. Things as practical as our purchases and way more important things like our calling, mission and legacy. If we just reached a bit higher, we would achieve results that spoke of excellence and not mediocrity. Doesn't

God deserve our very best? The truth is He does and He has given each of us the tools to equip ourselves for delivering exactly that.

And how about our faith? The Word of God tells us to study to show ourselves approved (2 Timothy 2:15) and to be like the Bereans (Acts 17) who daily searched the Word looking for truth. Why do you think that is? Knowledge for knowledge sake? No. It's way more important than that and summed up in one word: application. Knowledge fueled by the Holy Spirit gives us the ability to carry out our mission on earth; the ability to close the loop on what we started, knowing that we completed that assignment having given God and others our very best.

Quality Trumps Quantity

There was a time in my life where quantity was competing with quality in a dangerous way. Volume was sometimes valued more than holding to a high standard that didn't allow for finishing early. Good enough may get you through the door of completion but it won't be enough to get you through the door of highest opportunity. Proverbs 22:29 says "Do you see a man skillful in his work? He will stand before kings; he will not stand before obscure men." This is not about climbing a corporate ladder, it's about reaching the heights God has ordained for each of us to finish the race well. Philippians 3:14 makes it clear, "I press toward the goal for the prize of the upward call of God in Christ Jesus."

Recalibrate yourself to leave "good enough" behind and adopt a strong posture of upward thinking. Figuratively speaking if you are going to die on a hill, may it be a majestic mountain that taught you new things and will beckon you back, not that familiar low berm where average is widely celebrated. Drink in greatness and greatness will ooze out of you in every area of life. You can do it because He said you can! Push your Good to Better and your Better to Best in everything you do. Be all that God wants you to be and know that the greatest joy will come from knowing that you gave God your absolute best, over and over again!

"Healing and reconciliation depend on
how deep the wound, how far the root
of deception has burrowed in and how quickly
people will turn their hearts back to God."

Restoration

HAYWIRE

When life seems to go crazy, it's barely manageable and everything has sprung into a big mess...it's gone haywire. Funny how that expression quietly snuck into my speech at a very young age and hasn't left yet. Sometimes the tangled situation resembles fishing line backlashing on your old bait caster, when you failed to stop the motion of the spool with your thumb, before your lure hit the water. But sometimes your conundrum is really bad, like spools and spools of ornery wire wound under tension, springing into an uncontrollable snarl. Whatever it is it's no fun.

I was maybe 7 years old when my Uncle Joe brought a very cool Italian-made electric car home. I can remember riding that thing up and down the sidewalk like I was on some twisty road in the Dolomites with a flat top cap and a red scarf flying behind me in the wind. One day my friend Danny came by and with every bit of wide eyed sugared up kid passion, convinced me that we should take the electric motor out and replace it with a gas motor so we could have a real race car. Well, I bought the idea and pretty soon we were pulling parts out of that car left and right. We used a few appropriate tools but whenever the removal of something gave us a problem, we went for the hammer, which, by the way, became our favorite. By the time we were done there were mangled parts big and small everywhere. Wish you were there when dad came home. He took a look, and I'm sure with great restraint said, "you boys better put that thing back together."

Danny and I stood there, hammers in hand, totally stumped. It's one thing when things go haywire on their own, but we authored this one. Putting it back together wasn't an option but it was a lesson learned.

Only God Can Pull Us Back to Center

When things go haywire it can be an annoyance but when people go haywire it can be a tragedy. From time to time, as we do marriage counseling for others, Diana and I come across a spouse that, well, goes a bit crazy. This phenomenon is not gender specific. Diana calls it an alien abduction. As if they got hijacked to the spaceship and came back looking like themselves but are a totally different person. Pulling them back to center is something only God can do. 1 Corinthians 14:33a reminds us that "God isn't the author of confusion...". It's like they became disconnected to God...even though He was still with them, they were no longer listening, and confusion set in.

So what do we do when things like this happen to those we love... how do we help untangle the mess. The first thing to always remember is that our counsel needs to be wrapped in genuine love and kindness or it will fall on deaf ears. People who are in trouble, and have walked away from God's way, have already tuned out anything that would hinder them from continuing on their sinful path.

Romans 2:4 says "Or do you think lightly of the riches of His kindness and tolerance and patience, not knowing that the kindness of God leads you to repentance?" (NASB) It's easy for our concern to turn to anger. That's one of the many cards the enemy plays when we are trying to undo his evil work in the life of another. Remember, Satan holds a full deck of deception...that's his job and nobody does it better. We need to meditate on God's Word while taking captive every thought that would slow down the reconciliation process. We have to know Satan's schemes and not let any of them cloud our focus.

Winning a Fight at Any Cost Is Not the Goal

Many times one word, facial expression or body language can shatter peace, and pit one person against another. This is especially true if two people are quite alike. In this situation phrases like "take the high road" or "be the better person" are the motivators that we hope we all would adopt. For some it's easy, but for others this healing posture seems to butt up against our fighting nature. The enemy deceives us into thinking that winning a fight at any cost is the goal. One person gone haywire is bad enough, but two makes the reconciliation trickier and longer to bring about.

It takes two to fight, but if one is willing, there's a better chance that things will improve. The timing on this is so unpredictable. It's actually all over the map. Healing and reconciliation depend on how deep the wound, how far the root of deception has burrowed in and how quickly people will turn their hearts back to God. Many know the truth and that the truth can set them free. But they first have to want to be free and do the work. What's fighting against them is the human condition which provides a counterfeit sense of freedom as they exercise free will and do whatever they want.

Sometimes the person that went haywire isn't even willing to engage with anyone to at least get a second opinion on what went wrong. In that case we ramp up our prayer and, in the case of the believer, trust God that the good work He began will be completed

(Philippians 1:6) . Regarding an unbeliever, we pray and believe that the good work will begin with a heart change. Prayer isn't a last resort, it should be engaged always (Luke 18:1). Praying without ceasing (1 Thessalonians 5:16-18) is critical for ALL we do...for everything (Philippians 4:6)!

Speaking of prayer, my prayer for all of us is that our haywire is nothing more than benign annoyances and mild frustrations. And better yet, lets pray that our only knowledge of haywire is the ornery stuff they use to bale hay. So, with faith in your heart, move forward loving God and others and trust that restoration will surely follow.

"The 'little battles' we win each day,
the ones nobody but Jesus sees, are the battles
that give us the heavy artillery we need
for winning the big battle around the corner."

Perseverance

"THE SECRET WEAPON": WINNING THE BATTLE V/S DELIVERANCE

It's interesting to me that many of us, when it comes to our challenges, are waiting for deliverance. We don't realize the full value in winning the daily battle to overcome strongholds in our lives. Can God deliver us from our weaknesses and temptations? Absolutely! And, I agree that is what we should hope for. However, we can't forget that winning the battle one day at a time is a very good and mighty thing, and often exactly the way God delivers us! And, it's the encouragement we need to fight another day.

Proverbs 13:12 tells us: "Hope deferred makes the heart sick, but a longing fulfilled is a tree of life." So, let's hope for all that God has for us in a day to day kind of way. That's the "secret weapon" so many are missing today! Winning one battle at a time, knowing that by doing so, we will ultimately win the war.

Our Identity Is In Christ, Not What We Struggle With

I have a friend who struggled with alcohol. He wasn't just a social drinker but someone who used alcohol to self-medicate. Fortunately, he viewed himself not strictly as an alcoholic, but as a follower of Jesus Christ who struggled with alcohol. There's a profound difference. Was he an alcoholic in practical terms? Probably. But regarding who he was, he took the approach based on God's truth, that his identity was in Christ and not in something he struggled with. Now, this close friend was a regular AA (Alcoholics Anonymous) attender. And before you assume that I am speaking against Alcoholics Anonymous, let me be very clear. Programs that help people stay on the straight and narrow, keep their jobs, honor their families and are built on Godly principles are good with me. But along with AA, my friend knew the importance of understanding and professing Christ as his identity, as opposed to his addiction. The organization

Celebrate Recovery is another great resource, and its foundation is based wholly on our identity in Christ. The great benefit of this "identity first" approach is that it positions us to strengthen who we are in Christ and posture ourselves to fight from a place of victory.

Some people want something so bad they can't be happy unless they get it. Me, I'm a window shopper. I can be just as content looking at something as having it in my possession. That thought works pretty well if you are talking about a pair of new pants or maybe a new appliance. But when it comes to getting a monkey off your back for good it just doesn't work the same. That thought will work however, if your daily victories help keep you pointed in the right direction, and you have faith in a God that provides freedom.

Ultimately Your Victory Comes Through His Faithfulness

Many of us look at the enormity of whatever battle we are facing and focus on the giant task required to be rid of that thing once and for all. Alcohol, drugs, anger, fear, depression, sexual brokenness, whatever. Sometimes I wonder if we are just overwhelmed at the big looming on-going problem in our lives. Or if we use the thought, that the issue is too great to overcome, to sin one more time and then one more time again. "This is too big, I just can't do it." Well, the truth is, you do have a part to play in your healing and recovery, but God is there for you and ultimately your victory comes through His faithfulness. "It's not by might nor by power but by my Spirit says the LORD of Hosts" (Zechariah 4:6).

Think about it. How bad do we want to get over our problem? Bad enough to take small daily victories as encouragement? Or do we let the familiarity of the issue become a comfort? I know these are hard questions to ask. But if we want freedom and growth, we need to take the opportunity to do a thorough self-examination.

Let's say that you, like myself, hope for freedom, but welcome and actually rejoice in seemingly small daily victories. Winning the war one skirmish, one battle at a time! It's going to take perseverance to overcome discouragement and stay the course, even in the midst of your hopefulness and positive attitude. Perseverance is steady persistence in a course of action, a purpose, a state of being, etc., especially in spite of difficulties, obstacles, or discouragement. Sounds like our lives, right? We wish it were all just a walk in the park, but the reality of living on the planet includes struggles. The good news is, God equips us to overcome those things that hinder us. He is with us through it all. Take a look at 2 Corinthians 9:8: "God is able to make all grace abound to you, so that having all sufficiency in all things at all times, you may abound in every good work." And Isaiah 41:13: "For I am the LORD your God who takes hold of your right hand and says to you, Do not fear; I will help you."

Steady persistence in a course of action is the key strategy! Galatians 6:9 puts it this way: "And let us not grow weary while doing good, for in due season we shall reap if we do not lose heart."

So, what should our course of action be? One thing I would suggest is the greatest of all the commandments; "Love God with all your heart, with all your soul and with all your mind" Matthew 22:37. Loving God is the first step towards persevering. Keeping our eyes on Him and trusting that He will complete the good work that's started, will keep us on a straight path. And the second is like it "Love your neighbor as yourself" Matthew 22:39. That's where your support system comes from. God loves community and it's in that unity we will find strength to carry on. We were never meant to do life alone. As we love others, that love will always come back our way. That's the beauty of sowing and reaping.

That popular Rolling Stones song of the 60's reminds me of the way we can feel if we don't let small daily victories encourage us on our way to total healing. "I can't get no satisfaction." My daily satisfaction comes from knowing that I have done my part and trusted the One who sees my efforts and has me on His course and in His will. It comes from the hope I have in Christ and in His Word. And most of all it comes from knowing "...He who began a good work in you (me) will carry it on to completion until the day of Christ Jesus" Phil 1:6. We have to actively believe this, take it to heart. The "little battles" we win each day, the ones nobody but Jesus sees, are the battles that give us the heavy artillery we need for winning the big battle around the corner. That and knowing that the Holy Spirt will lead and guide us keeps us confidently moving forward.

Carry on my friends, trusting the promised hope for deliverance, yet rejoicing in the daily victories that come from a heart of obedience. Love God and live a life of perseverance. Stay the course, one foot in front of the other and one victory at a time no matter how small it may seem. When you live faithfully like that, you can watch and be amazed at all that it adds up to. The Lord will join you in battle as you persevere and overcome one day, one battle, at a time!

"If we keep our hearts and minds open
to people's needs we will get better
at identifying those needs and choosing
the right words to speak into those lives."

Encouragement

ELEVEN

STRONG MEDICINE

"But encourage one another daily,
as long as it is called 'Today,' so that none of you
may be hardened by sin's deceitfulness."
— Hebrews 3:13 NIV

Have you ever watched someone's face change when you speak words of life to them? What a privilege it is to get to change someone's day from gloomy to bright with just a few simple words. Proverbs 18:21 tells us that "Death and life are in the power of the tongue, And those who love it will eat its fruit." Every one of us has that power within our own vocabulary. Be purposeful in looking for opportunities to encourage others. If we keep our hearts and minds open to people's needs we will get better at identifying those needs and choosing the right words to speak into those lives.

We've all been on the receiving end of hurtful words and some of those words have stuck with us throughout our lives. Often, we replay those lies over and over, bringing needless worry into our lives like a poison that we keep drinking. We end up in counseling, handicapped, and unsuccessful in relationships because of the lies delivered by someone else's careless and mean-spirited speech. It's time to start the healing, first in our delivery of encouragement to others and then in the rebound that comes from that delivery back to us. "Worry weighs a person down; an encouraging word cheers a person up" (Proverbs 12:25 NLT).

A Beautiful Cycle of Blessing

We need to remember that "…the joy of the LORD is your strength" Nehemiah 8:10b. One of the easiest ways to help people become and stay strong in the Lord is to encourage them. What a great habit to develop. Not only will you lift someone's spirits, but it will come right back to you with the same power that it was given. It's a beautiful cycle of blessing others and being blessed in return.

Many times, people like myself with a dominant creative bent can be a bit more fragile when it comes to our craft. Our skin is a little thinner. We receive compliments with more enthusiasm and criticism with more worry. We can be way up one minute and way down the next.

While we can't control what other people will say or how they will say it, we can certainly make sure that we are always sensitive to others with our words and delivery. If we want to receive the best from others, we need to give others the best from us. 2 Corinthians 9:6 says "But this I say: He who sows sparingly will also reap sparingly, and he who sows bountifully will also reap bountifully." Isn't a bountiful life the kind of life we want to live? God has made this available to us. If we truly believe it, 2 Corinthians 9:6 guarantees it! We WILL reap what we sow.

Other than the continual encouragement from my wife Diana and our kids, probably one of the most memorable compliments I have ever received came from my dad. A musician who inspired me to walk in his footsteps, he remains one of the best encouragers I have ever known. Not because of his words alone, but because of the love those words were wrapped in.

Transported to a New Place

I was about 30 years old playing at a local club, when dad walked in and listened to our set. From the downbeat forward, it seemed like any other night, but the words from my father changed everything. His words have remained in my heart and have been replayed many times over. Dad had heard me play with various bands many times, but to him I had turned a corner. While my growth as a musician was gradual, his encouragement that night made me feel like I had been quickly transported to a new place, a place that I had targeted for myself many years before. I remember where we were standing, the joy I felt in hearing his enthusiastic praise and what those words have done for me in the decades that followed. That's what encouragement does...that's what love does!

I realize how blessed I am. I also know there are many who can't tell this same type of story. While we can't change history, we can change the future starting now. Whether our motivation comes from passing along the encouragement we have received, or making sure others benefit from something we haven't received ourselves, let's all be encouragers. Not with empty words but with powerful words. Words that are put together from a compassionate heart, delivered and sown with honesty and love. That kind of strong medicine, when freely poured out, will always bring a healthy return.

"When your priorities aren't right anything can happen. It takes a good inward look to see where you are in life and then the fortitude to persevere through a revamping that will change everything."

Growth

TWELVE

TIME TO DANCE

Figuring out how to live with old regrets is something most of us have had to do. Some regrets are easy to leave behind but some hang on like a foul smell that gets in your nose hairs and follows you around. Sure, God can deliver us from that sadness. But many times, the memory of our bad judgment goes into the back of a filing cabinet in our mind, only to worm its way forward at times as a reminder of our misguided past. Every one of us has said something we wish we didn't say and done something we wish we didn't do. That's just a symptom of our imperfect life. But for every mistake we have made there's most always a way to make it right.

Not long ago I was at a wedding reception that had a great dance band. The energy in the room was electric, and everyone was celebrating the new couple by joining in on the dance floor. Lots of smiles, laughter and general good vibes all around. What really caught my eye was a table of four or five musicians attending the wedding who were just sitting there while their wives were out on the wooden floor basically dancing with each other. Sure, the girls were having fun, but I knew they would have loved it if their men were out there with them.

As a musician I remember how much easier it was to make the music rather than being a member of the audience enjoying it. We loved being musicians, loved being in our tribe, but for some strange reason some of us were either afraid, too self-conscious or embarrassed to just have fun. Believe it or not a lot of musicians have a bit of an introverted personality that really shows up when we are not on stage. It wouldn't seem that way but many times it's true.

This isn't just a musician thing. This social syndrome of arrested development can hit anyone. It's especially present when you work at your gifts and talents like a madman, leaving little time or interest for the rest of life. When your priorities aren't right anything can happen. It takes a good inward look to see where you are in life and then the fortitude to persevere through a revamping that will change everything. It's easy to briefly live deceived and even easier to just stay that way, especially if you aren't seeking first God's Kingdom and His righteousness. Matthew 6:33 says; "But seek first His kingdom and His righteousness, and all these things will be added to you." (NASB)

So, what are "these things"? We can start with material things such as food, clothing and shelter, but good sense and a desire to grow must be on the list somewhere!

Fearless in Our World
but Fearful in Everyone Else's

In my world, as long as I had my bass guitar strapped on, I was fearless. If I had to put it down and just speak or interact with non-creative types I was a fish out of water. It scared me to death. While most young men were figuring out how to navigate social situations, many musicians hid behind their instruments and let their talent and the accolades they got from it become their identity. In some ways we thought we were exempt from normal living. But when the time came to figure out regular life our perceived exemption became our snag. That happens to many of us, including doctors, nurses, carpenters, businesspersons, even stay at home parents. We can all hide behind or within our careers and vocations, where we know our stuff, and have our own tribe who know us. In a sense some of us become stunted, handicapped and struggling just to be contenders in "normal" life. Fearless in our world but fearful in everyone else's.

"Fear of man will prove to be a snare, but whoever trusts in the LORD is kept safe" (Proverbs 29:25 NIV).

But finally, with the direction of our faithful God, His Holy Spirit and other people filled with Godly wisdom and love, we hopefully wake up. Somehow and some way, if our eyes are fixed on Christ, the things that are important in life will trump all the other less important and even dysfunctional things. Every under-thought-out career driven desire, those things that made it easy for us to postpone growing up, even that false sense of being better off in our own specialized world all fade. Responsibility that seemed like an undesirable option becomes the brass ring. We get to a point where we desperately need it! It's the stability that helps keep us on God's course and even legitimizes some of the things in our life that took us off course in the first place. The sweet spot of God's will and purpose for our lives draws us in like a tractor beam pulling us to a brave new world.

Sometimes Speaking the Truth Involves Taking a Risk

So, that brings us back to the wedding with the table of musicians probably talking about gear and gigs while their wives were having fun. They could have been me and my bandmates decades ago. Happy to be musicians and mostly getting that right but leaving some of the rest of life on the table to be figured out at a later date.

Getting more comfortable in my own skin with every passing year, I confidently approached their table and sat down. After some small talk and introductions, I went there: "Guys...don't do what I did when I was your age. No matter how hard it may seem, get up and shock the heck out of your wives. Just go out there and dance. All you have to do is smile and move, nothing fancy or complicated. You all have rhythm, so go and make your wives happy now, so you won't have to make up for lost time later."

Well, I must have made a big impression on them because...they did absolutely nothing! Probably thought I was nuts; just an older guy with something to say. Yet, I hold on to the Biblical fact that when you speak a truth based directly or even loosely on God's word or a Godly principle, it doesn't return void (Isaiah 55:11).

Is life in front of you with everyone in it, and you are stuck sitting at the table on the edge of all the action? If it is, and you are...put on your dancing shoes and jump in. No looking back. It's good for you, blesses God and it's great for those you love. It's time to dance and you're the dancer...own it, do it, love it!

"The power that lives within a song

is available to all of us. Whether we write them,

play them or just listen, we are all

affected by their impact."

Inspiration

GREAT SONGS DO THAT

Great songs do something amazing to me. The right song at the right time moves me to change, to repent, to worship, to cheer up, to get motivated, to do God's will, to just plain enjoy the day!

Great Songs Help Us Live Out God's Word

There's hardly an end to what great songs do. They are a teacher, a leader, they bring strength, bring joy, they're an invitation, they help you live out God's Word, they stir us up, and they are a seed that leads to salvation. Songs are so needed and there's rarely a person that doesn't appreciate a great one. Whether you are a listener, a songwriter a musician or all three great songs make up the soundtrack of our lives.

I was having a visit with a friend the other day when something he said triggered a song title. Three words and some inspiration were all I had. Throughout the day I pondered my new title and began developing the verses in my mind. It was a touching thought and the verses would follow someone through a lifetime. From a young age to that transitional time when we believers pass from earthly life to eternal life. At the end of the day I briefly shared the title and idea with my wife Diana. Immediately we both teared up. I knew I had something good brewing.

Our reaction was just from a title and an idea. I probably only spoke a few brief sentences of description. No music, no melody, no chord changes, rhythm, vibey production or finished lyrics. Again, just a title and a thought.

God's Anointing and Our Diligence Will Produce Great Songs

Just to be clear, that doesn't happen with every song we write. But when it does happen, I believe, with God's anointing and our diligence, great songs will follow. That's why songwriters write isn't it? In hopes of hitting upon something universal that will move people. This truth applies for all of us, whatever gifts, talents and roles God has us in: When you have a solid foundation to build on, with care and concern, the rest of your efforts will make something beautiful and touch many. In the same way our foundation in Christ lends itself, actually leads us, to a relationship with Him that produces fruit and reproduces itself in others.

In the case of the Christian songwriter, some of that fruit should be great songs. Songs that move people in the direction of God. Songs that reflect the fruit of the Spirit. Songs that speak to the human condition celebrating that which lines up to the Word and thoughtfully offering instruction for that which does not.

When you begin with a strong idea and lyric, as I mentioned above, you're off to a great start. But, once the song is finished and every element comes together the listener is touched, and music does that thing that you, the writer, hope for. A great song goes deep into your being, connecting with everything that makes us both human and Spirit beings.

Great Songs Are a Delivery Vehicle to Great Memories

Just think about it...how many times has a certain song taken you to a memory that you love to relive? It happens to every one of us and we love it when it does. Sometimes it's one single thought and other times it's a flood of memories, people's faces and the recollection of great times gone by. Great songs are a delivery vehicle to your fondest memories.

A Christian musician, writer or artist has the opportunity to influence people in everything from life-changing ways to the simplest of happy reflective moments. And… you don't even have to be there!

Calling, responsibility, passion, and the knowledge that if great music is in you, it has to come out, will propel you to the wonderful fulfillment of your destiny as a creative being with a musical bent. When you combine all the elements of great music into each song you write or choose to play, something happens exponentially that is really out of your control. The player and the listener come together to ignite something in the listener's heart and mind that makes a statement…an impact of great value.

Mostly We Play Songs That Move Us

If you are not a writer, the care you put into picking songs for worship or your band's next gig or the playlist you listen to will yield the very same result. Mostly we play songs that move us. When was the last time you picked a song to play that you didn't like? Other than when someone in authority asked you to. In that situation, by the way, play it like you love it because there is usually a reason that song was suggested. Play it, listen to it and see what God will do.

The power that lives within a song is available to all of us. Whether we write them, play them or just listen, we are all affected by their impact. With all of who King David was, being a Psalmist was a huge piece of his DNA. He knew the gift God gave him and he used it wisely in his lifetime. Discover your musical gifts and musical tastes all for God's glory!

"Love is the main ingredient

in earning the right to say the hard stuff

to people who are a bit out of balance."

Love

FOURTEEN

LOVE WILL BE THE WEAPON

In today's world it seems everything can turn into a weapon for those who are always looking for a fight. Music, books, movies the local and national media, social media, etc. If we are not careful we can easily get drawn into everyone's offense and be wound up tight in an argument with no end. But I have not seen anything melt away anger, frustration, hurt feelings, wrong assumptions and misunderstandings like love. Love does something nothing else can. It seeps into our innermost being and says everything will work out, I am loved, God's got it. We are encouraged in 1 Peter 4:8 to love each other deeply because "love covers a multitude of sins."

Whenever we see a long term or even lifetime friendship, it developed because love was involved. Love was at the forefront speaking loudly in the midst of two people getting to know each other.

Love not only shows itself in ongoing relationships but in one-off encounters. I remember being at a rental car counter, third in line, as I witnessed two people in front of me get so angry with the woman behind the counter because something, beyond her control, didn't work out the way they had hoped. The woman did everything she could to remain calm and professional but was visibly shaken. When it was my turn, her greeting was stern, cool and reflected her anticipation that I was going to be one more rude, unkind customer just like the last two. God was already working in me and I was just the opposite. I showed kindness, told her what an amazing job she did in dealing with the angry men, and before long we were showing each other pictures of our kids! I got an upgrade, by the way, which was totally not my motive, but another good thing that comes forth when we love God and others.

Mark 12:28b-31 speaks to the importance of love with the most authority. "Of all the commandments, which is the most important?" "The most important one," answered Jesus, "is this: 'Hear, O Israel: The Lord our God, the Lord is one. Love the Lord your God with all your heart and with all your soul and with all your mind and with all your strength.' The second is this: 'Love your neighbor as yourself.' There is no commandment greater than these." (NIV)

Winning the Argument Isn't Always the Goal

Do you ever notice, during times of confrontation, coming away from the verbal exchange feeling discouraged? I would guess more times than not this was when you entered in to the conversation trying to win the argument rather than prayerfully listening for God's solution and wrapping every word in love. On the contrary when you use love to diffuse anger and anxiety, no matter the outcome, you can leave in peace knowing you did what God wanted you to do. Many times, reconciliation comes, but when it doesn't you can know that God was pleased with your part and you can trust Him with the rest.

There is a difference between passionately defending a Godly position with authority and resolve and letting harsh words in your conversation position you as a know it all and maybe even a bully. Passion can quickly turn to anger if you are not guarded. Believe me, a soapbox defense can quickly turn bad if you are not filled up with God's love in perfect balance with His truth. The unfortunate thing in these cases is the very people who need to hear what you are saying will tune out because of the lack of love in your delivery. This happens all the time. That lost opportunity may not come around again.

Love is the main ingredient in earning the right to say the hard stuff to people who are a bit out of balance.

How do I know this? Because I have been out of balance many times and the people I trust, who I know love me, have gently set me straight. Oh, make no mistake, there have been raised voices and strong words at times. But the love that was evident was always the delivery vehicle that allowed me to receive the good instruction and not run from it.

Sometimes we may only have one chance to pass along words of encouragement or correction to someone. Usually, if we are listening, the Holy Spirit makes it evident if someone needs to hear something from God through us. Personally, I can move quickly on words of encouragement. After all, who doesn't want to hear those. It's the words of correction that truly take more discernment and thought.

Love Settles Hearts

Possibly you have found yourself the mediator in an uncomfortable situation. This is another example of needing to let God's love marinate in your heart before you speak. In an emotional stand-off let that, intermingled with your discernment for the right solution bring peace. In this and every conundrum that you find yourself, be prayed up, always bring comfort, and above all create an atmosphere of love that is so strong it's impossible to miss. Anglican clergyman, Hugh Richard Lawrie said, "Love is the only weapon we need." In books, songs and quotations, people have been ascribing to that incredible truth since it was first written.

My prayer for us all is that we come to the Lord each day, and in every circumstance, asking Him to fill us with His love. I pray we take every opportunity in our lives, whether part of our daily routine or something out of the blue, to let our great love for God and others shine through.

Let's take a moment to pray: Lord, please fill us with your Holy Spirit as we find ourselves in situations of conflict. Let us pour ourselves out to You and those You put in our path armed with love above all. Amen!

"We have a Supervisor who keeps us close,

teaches us and encourages us as we go.

He is always with us and will always be

our biggest champion."

Authority

WHO'S YOUR SUPERVISOR?

Not long ago I went to the Home Depot to get a few things. Screw anchors, light bulbs, duct tape, that sort of stuff. When I entered the store, I was welcomed by the greeter and about twenty feet away from him was a fella who was promoting heating and cooling services. He was a young guy whose mission I suppose was to pitch his services to customers and hopefully sign them up for what he was offering.

Well, the guy barely looked at me, didn't smile and certainly didn't try to sell me anything. He looked pretty bored, and I was actually glad he didn't try to sell me, because I didn't need what he was selling. I carried on with my shopping and when I was nearly finished, passed him by one more time. This time, however, he had a guy standing next to him, older, more buttoned down and obviously his supervisor. When the young salesman saw me, he lit up and started his spiel. Pleasant, detailed, and although not overly aggressive, serious and deliberate for sure. I politely thanked him, said I was all set and made my way to the checkout.

When I walked out of the store, I think I chuckled out loud thinking of the huge difference in that guy when his supervisor was present. Wow, I thought, how different would we all be if our supervisor was with us every minute of every day. Then it dawned on me, He is!

> HE IS WITH YOU ALWAYS: "And surely I am with you always, to the very end of the age." (Matthew 28:20b NIV)

> HE SEES ALL: "The eyes of the LORD are everywhere, keeping watch on the wicked and the good." (Proverb 15:3 NIV)

> HE IS YOUR FRIEND: "I no longer call you servants, because a servant does not know his master's business. Instead, I have called you friends, for everything that I learned from my Father I have made known to you." (John 15:15 NIV)

We have a constant companion and a faithful friend with Jesus. He is always with us to see our successes, failures, good judgment and bad. While we know this in our head, do our actions reflect this reality or are we, like many, conveniently forgetful? Especially when we are not behaving well.

> HE IS YOUR SAVIOR: "But grow in the grace and knowledge of our Lord and Savior Jesus Christ. To Him be glory both now and forever! Amen." (2 Peter 3:18 NIV)

> HE HAS YOUR BEST INTERESTS IN MIND: "For I know the plans I have for you," declares the Lord, "plans to prosper you and not to harm you, plans to give you hope and a future." (Jeremiah 29:11 NIV)

He Is Worthy of All Praise

"Great is the Lord and most worthy of praise; His greatness no one can fathom." (Psalm 145:3 NIV) Now that's a supervisor! Our compassionate Savior wanting only His very best for us, and so worthy of our adoration and praise.

Do everything in Christ and know that He's not a God that peers over your shoulder waiting for you to blow it. He's a God who loves you, encourages you, does everything He can to help you reach your goals and wants only goodness for you.

We serve a merciful Savior who is also a righteous Judge. Our God loves us through this life and will judge our actions at the end of our earthly life. What we settle into career wise, and more importantly, as believers just doing life with those we love and whose paths we cross, all should reflect the heart of our God and line up to the instruction He gives us through His Word. We need to pray daily for a fresh filling of the Holy Spirit, in order to be discerning as we move through each day making our choices.

"Nothing in all creation is hidden from God's sight. Everything is uncovered and laid bare before the eyes of Him to whom we must give account." (Hebrews 4:13 NIV)

The time we spend meditating on God's Word and communing with Him throughout the day is directly related to how aware of His presence we are. Not just knowing He's there, but sensing Him in a tangible way. Though invisible, His presence can really be felt, and that reality can and will keep us focused on Him and living life well all the time.

He Is Your Keeper

"The LORD is your keeper; the LORD is your shade at your right hand. The sun shall not strike you by day, nor the moon by night. The LORD shall preserve you from all evil; He shall preserve your soul. The LORD shall preserve your going out and your coming in from this time forth, and even forevermore." (Psalm 121:5-8)

Now, back to our young salesman friend at the Home Depot. If he realized that he was entrusted with a responsibility, whether or not he was under his boss's watchful eye, his actions would have been consistent even when he was on his own. Hopefully that's a lesson he has learned and one we have learned related to God and living a life of integrity in every situation. If we believe the Word of God to be true, we are never alone. We have a Supervisor who keeps us close, teaches us and encourages us as we go. He is always with us and will always be our biggest champion. You won't ever have to look far for Him because He not only walks with us, He is in us. And who could have a better supervisor than the Lover of Our Soul!

"Don't ever underestimate the power
of your words and your work to bring
hope and inspiration to others."

SIXTEEN

OUR RESPONSIBILITY
OF INFLUENCE

Most of us feel the need to share good stuff with others. We get great joy from passing on the name of a great restaurant, a movie, a new song or artist or some wonderful person someone just has to meet. At the top of that list, actually on a list all by itself, is the name Jesus. As we remember the Great Commission, hopefully we are compelled to tell people what He means to us, who He is and what He will mean to them when they get to know Him.

The key to this kind of influence is nurturing relationships. Celebrating others and making people feel good about themselves when they are with us is foundational. Do we make people feel like they are the only ones on the planet when we speak to them? Even with strangers, in a few minutes of connection, you can make them feel good about who they are. Many times, this will open the door for sharing nuggets of truth about your Savior.

American author, speaker, and pastor John Maxwell said, "the amount of influence you have on another person is directly related to how good they feel about themselves when they are in your company." That's certainly on my list of top 5 favorite quotes. Nothing is truer than that when it comes to the weight your words will carry in someone's life.

Your Work and Your Words Carry Weight

Besides connecting with people in direct face to face conversation, our work speaks volumes as well. Salesperson, stay-at-home mom, business manager, landscaper, lawyer, or in my case as a pastor, musician and songwriter, whatever our work, it makes a connection all by itself. The work we do and the way we conduct ourselves at it, reflects who we are, how we believe and what influences us. God is amazing, and He knows how to knit all the pieces together to bring about influence in people's lives. That influence is sparked into a fire directly by God. And that flame spreads through the lives of others propelling them forward in all they do.

Hopefully the way you go about your work is the result of your relationship with God which includes what you are hearing in your quiet times and what the Holy Spirit is impressing upon you regarding the people you work with. Knowing these two things will help you greatly as you diligently work to complete the tasks set before you. Colossians 3:23a says "Whatever you do, work at it with all your heart, as working for the Lord" (NIV) and Matthew 5:16 declares "let your light shine before others, that they may see your good deeds and glorify your Father in heaven." (NIV) We not only have an audience of One, we have an audience of many!

Don't ever underestimate the power of your words and your work to bring hope and inspiration to others. Think about what happens in your own heart when you recall something wonderful that someone said to you, or you feel the satisfaction that comes from having done a good job. When something flows through you that was inspired by your commitment to God, it touches others in many ways that God uses for his purposes.

Another blessing that comes from this kind of influence is not only what it does to the recipient, but what it does as it spills over to someone else. Consider Timothy's words in 2 Timothy 2:2 "And the things you have heard me say in the presence of many witnesses entrust to reliable people who will also be qualified to teach others." (NIV) Influence lives in the most beautiful way; in the moment and through a lifetime in the hearts, minds and lives of others.

By His Blood and the Word of Our Testimony

Whether at work, or simply living your day to day looking for opportunities to bless and encourage others, YOUR life tells a story. Revelation 12:11 tells us "And they overcame him (Satan, our enemy) by the blood of the Lamb and by the word of their testimony, and they did not love their lives to the death." We overcome by the blood of the Lamb and the word of OUR testimony. Jesus went to the cross because of His love for us. Now, because of our love for Him, we can share a testimony that will change others and help us AND them to overcome the evil one in the process.

As you start each day, ask God to pour His love through you and out to others in every situation. Determine not to go anywhere in your mind that would hinder that. If you feel a counterproductive posture creeping in, take that thought captive to the obedience of Christ (2 Corinthians 10:5) and pray it away so you can spread God's love to others and always have influence on them for the things that matter.

We are all influencers. May our words, work and lives be an outward expression of the inward work God continues to do in us. Lord, may it be.

"You have a destiny, one that's designed by God. He has taken every bit of how He made you into consideration and gives you nudges along the way to set you or keep you on course."

Calling

SEVENTEEN

MEATBALLS AND VICARIOUS LIVING

I believe all of us live vicariously to one degree or another. Webster's Dictionary says this about the word vicarious: "Experienced or felt by watching, hearing about or reading about someone else instead of doing it yourself." My question is, does that second-hand experience motivate us to achieve our own goals, or simply satisfy us enough so we falsely believe that a moment of pleasure lived from the sidelines is all we need.

When It's Good

Ok, to be clear, living vicariously by mentoring another to reach their goals and full potential is great. There's no problem with that. Whether it's your child, another's, a friend or student, your immediate reward is celebrating their victories and successes as you watch them learn and grow. Wonderful. That's good for us, and good for them, to see our joy and approval.

Here is one of the many ways we celebrate others through teaching; The culinary crown jewel in our family is meatballs. This is no small thing. "How do you make your meatballs" is one of the most commonly asked questions from Italian to Italian—not kidding here— meatballs are a big deal! So, when our grandkids, Luke and Eva, were tall enough to stand on a stool and reach the kitchen counter the apron went on and the ingredients came out. The meat: everyday meatballs, use whatever you like or whatever is on sale, beef, beef and pork, even turkey (we can make it taste like beef) but, for special occasions, thirds of beef, pork and veal. Then the eggs, 2 for each pound of meat, grated cheese (not the cheap stuff), minced onion, garlic, parsley, bread-crumbs (or bread soaked in milk and rung out), salt, pepper, and whatever else makes them unique, i.e. your special ingredient. See what I did? I didn't tell you what our special ingredient is, but Luke and Eva know! And, some of you are already disagreeing with my recipe, I know you are.

Diana and I get great joy from teaching Luke and Eva how to do something we love. Watching them learn to crack the eggs, put the ingredients in, in varying or even ridiculous amounts...Ha! We watch them roll the meatballs...sized from marbles to the occasional softball and carefully place them in the frying pan. Then, the best part, they taste their creation, and it's always "can I have one more." The small bit of vicarious in this example is healthy, because we are in the experience by teaching and coaching. They learn while we feel their pleasure and our own.

When It's Not

The other side of the spectrum can be within the world of pageants, music and sports. Motivating our kids to develop their gifts is one thing but stage parents and bleacher quarterbacks, living their unfulfilled dreams through their kids, can sometimes aggressively push them to succeed in areas they may have little interest in. You've seen it; red faced parents raging at their kids with disapproval while these young ones listen with quivering lips and hearts filled with rejection. Other than the unnecessary trail of tears and years of future therapy, how else can vicarious living potentially hinder you from your full potential? Think of this:

You have a destiny, one that's designed by God. He has taken every bit of how He made you into consideration and gives you nudges along the way to set you or keep you on course. You have a dream, a goal, a hope for your life based on something you love and have passion for. Alongside of that, you have that familiar kind of fear that whispers to you you're not good enough, that it will never happen, there's no way. So, you find it easier and even safer to fulfill your desire through someone else success. And, that little bit of vicarious pleasure becomes the counterfeit experience that can rob you of God's best for your life.

This happens all the time. Professional counselors hear these stories day after day at $100.00 plus an hour. Relationships are taxed because you just can't get past the fact that you missed something, and life just isn't any fun. Why am I here, what am I made for, etc. Proverbs 13:12 reminds us that "Hope deferred makes the heart sick..." (NIV) and the sad part is, that deferred hope may have been avoided. The rest of that verse is "But when desire comes it is a tree of life".

Light Your Fire

While you may be able to enjoy a momentary emotional payoff through the career, calling, recreation or passion of another, true joy comes from doing it yourself in your area of desire, expertise and enthusiasm.

Things like discouragement, or lack of Godly confidence, can be the spark that lights the fire. The musician, for example, hears someone play that is more accomplished than they are and they jokingly quip "I'm never playing my instrument again". Unfortunately for some that casual comment may come to pass or at the least slow them down enough that their ramped up vicarious enjoyment trespasses on their time to improve and grow.

Every one of us has something that sets us apart. Some unique mix of personality, talent and gifting in percentages that were designed for each of us exclusively. Those things in our life we really enjoy. Things that, when we are doing them, we feel God's pleasure. There's not one, not even one life that doesn't have purpose either jumping out in front of them or anxiously waiting, just below the surface, for permission to launch.

As you move forward in life my hope for you is this; Go ahead, cheer your friends on, celebrate the accomplishments of others, but please, develop what God's given you, so that fresh victories and the drive to make them real, will forever be yours.

"The benefit of loving God and loving people is always the same; possessing the comforting knowledge that you are living life God's way and knowing that ALL are being blessed in the process."

Love

THAT'S WHAT LOVE DOES

Recently, while visiting family in our hometown of Syracuse NY, I had an interesting encounter with an elderly woman. While we were spending some time with my Mother-in-Law at a rehabilitation center, I was walking down a hallway on my way out of the building. I saw a woman in a wheel chair barely moving, head down and looking very sad and distant. I walked up to her and said, "How are you doing today?" She slowly and with much effort lifted her head, looked directly at me and said, "Not good!" Then almost without pause added, "I've been waiting for you…I need to go someplace." "Where do you want to go" I asked. "Wherever you want to take me," she said with a smile.

After a few more minutes I finished our brief chat and realized that although we can't always take people where they physically want to go, we can take them places through love with just a few words and a show of kindness.

THAT'S WHAT LOVE DOES
It Reaches Out and Pulls You In

That's a lyric from a song I co-wrote with Bob Halligan Jr. It jumped out at me and made me again realize that love transcends perceived obstacles, penetrates hard places of the heart and brings life back into the soul.

In my life I have realized repeatedly, that the single most effective weapon I have available to me for living life in Christ is love.

1 Corinthians 13:13 says "And now these three remain: faith, hope and love. But the greatest of these is love." (NIV)

How many times have we heard this verse? Over and over I'm sure. My question for us is; do we really know what love can do and how important God's message of love is to us all? When asked which the greatest commandment in the law is, In Matthew 22:37-39 Jesus replied, "'Love the Lord your God with all your heart and with all your soul and with all your mind.' This is the first and greatest commandment. And the second is like it: 'Love your neighbor as yourself.'" (NIV) Not just second to it, but like it!

The benefit of loving God and loving people is always the same; possessing the comforting knowledge that you are living life God's way and knowing that ALL are being blessed in the process.

We've all heard the saying "a smile is contagious." How true that is, but I would also add "love is contagious." To see love displayed through kindness not only brings a smile and warms you up, but also makes you want to duplicate it.

In 1 Peter 2:17 we read, "Honor all people. Love the brotherhood. Fear God. Honor the king." In this verse Peter encourages us to "fear God" and to honor everyone from "all people" and "the brotherhood" to "the king." Not only a good king or ruler who we respect but also the tyrants of that day. What would love do to THEM? On the surface maybe not much, but if we believe in the power of love and the importance of love, according to God and His word, there's more going on than we could imagine.

Love covers, love forgives, love protects, love encourages, love lifts up, love draws, love shares, love believes in, love sacrifices for, love goes above and beyond, and love puts others first. Romans 12:10 says "Be devoted to one another in love. Honor one another above yourselves." (NIV)

THAT'S WHAT LOVE DOES
It Takes Your Hand and Calls You Friend

We've all been there. You're at a party or an event, and there are groups of people talking and having a great time. But off to the side there's always someone looking like a fish out of water, or someone standing near, but not being included in the conversation. How awkward that must feel for them. I remember that feeling well, and many of you may remember it too. That's when you say to yourself (if just for a moment) "never again, never will I venture out of my comfort zone."

Truth is, we could change everything in that single moment for someone, if we decide to go into situations looking for people who are disconnected, bringing them in to the conversation and engaging them with interest. They will walk away feeling loved, and maybe even braver for their next encounter.

You Don't Have to Abandon One
to Look for Another

The real question is, are we willing to do the work of loving? It does take effort and there is a price. It's no different at church, work or school, where much of our joy comes from seeing our friends each week and getting to catch up a bit. That's great and needed, but don't forget to ask God for a connection to others that need us as well. You don't have to abandon one to look for another. I am fully convinced that in God's economy we can do it all and not miss a thing. There will be a difference though, a greater feeling of purpose and completeness at the end of the day. That's what love does!

"We have favor because of God and more of it

because of the way we implement God's ways

into all we do and in every relationship."

Favor

NINETEEN

GOD'S GIFT, OUR BLESSING

Hopefully I'm not the only one who has experienced the joy of favor. Favor is giving special regard to someone, treating someone with goodwill or showing exceptional kindness to someone. Psalm 5:12 says "For You, O LORD, will bless the righteous; With favor You will surround him as with a shield." What a wonderful thought. But who are the righteous? God's word says the righteous are you and I. Believers who put our faith and trust in Jesus. We are not without sin, but when we do sin, we quickly repent and get back on course (1 John 1:9). Because of, and in Jesus, we are the righteousness of

God (1 Corinthians 5:21). He made Him who knew no sin to be sin on our behalf, so that we might become the righteousness of God in Him. (2 Corinthians 5:22). It's an amazing truth, and it places believers within God's favor!

When you experience God's favor you know it. An act of kindness comes your way, an upgrade of some type, a great bargain beyond what you expected. It can be as simple as someone opening a door for you, letting you in a bumper to bumper lane of traffic or someone doing something noticeably more like sending you an anonymous check or picking up your dinner bill. My lovely wife Diana and I reference our "Parking Anointing" every time God gives us a prime spot. No matter how great or small, it's a blessing from God and always appreciated.

Favor Is God's Idea

I experience God's favor every morning when I wake up. Just to get out of bed is a gift, another day to be with The Lord and experience whatever He has lying ahead. Matthew 7:11 says "If you then, being evil, know how to give good gifts to your children, how much more will your Father who is in heaven give good things to those who ask Him!" Your simple prayer, the night before or the morning of, sets the stage for another day of favor, another day of walking with The King. Favor is God's idea and like everything that comes from Him, it's a good one!

God's favor can come directly from Him or it can come from others. It could come from someone who had a great relationship and because of it wants to pass kindness and favor along to another. Consider the story of Mephibosheth:

Mephibosheth was the son of Jonathan and had no good reason to expect kind treatment from King David. But, because of David's love for Jonathan, and a vow that David and Jonathan had made in 1 Samuel 20:14,15 favor came to Mephibosheth totally unexpected. In that vow Jonathan said "'And you shall not only show me the kindness of the LORD while I still live, that I may not die; but you shall not cut off your kindness from my house forever...'"

So later on, in 2 Samuel 9:1 David asks if there is still anyone who is left of the house of Saul, that I may show him kindness for Jonathan's sake?" And there it is! God's favor being bestowed on others because of the love and friendship that was sown many years prior.

Favor Can Be Generational

As a young boy I received God's favor from others as well. I didn't earn it, work for it or necessarily deserve it. Yet it rested on me because of the good ground my relatives laid throughout their lives. I can remember being with my grandfather feeling love and kindness from others because of how they were treated by him as they worked together to build a successful car dealership. I knew them all, from the sales guys to the mechanics. My grandfather would always stop and talk to them about their families, their kids...just anything. He treated everyone with respect and because of that, love not only came his was way, but mine as well. I literally can remember them leaning down with big smiles to talk to me. They made me feel good...favored.

I could go on and on about some of my relatives and hopefully yours too, folks who loved people and made them feel honored and good about themselves. Through that our families set us up for much favor in our lives. Again, not earned or worked for, given simply because the people in our lives poured into others. Oh, they weren't perfect to be sure but they loved and respected people. For those who participated this was at the top of their list and instilled for a lifetime in us all. By the way, if your family never showed you much love or favor, when you are part of God's family, he'll never drop that ball. Being in God's family means sharing in His favor! It's His gift to us, it comes with Salvation!

When we give ourselves to others, others give themselves to us. Not always, of course, but when relationships function as they should that's what happens. We have favor because of God and more of it because of the way we implement God's ways into all we do and in every relationship. We have it ALL with God, unmerited and unearned, but because we love Him so much, we don't leave it at that. We dig deeper, we reach higher for love's sake. Although the benefit is not our motive, the benefit comes. Better relationships, more favor, and more life.

When God pours His favor on us it comes in many different ways but all from Him. He is the source. He will bless us—we who've been made righteous by God's grace—and surround us with favor. We can trust God for favor. We can live life gratefully for what's already been given to us by God directly, supernaturally and through the good living of others. And let's put every Godly principle into action in our lives as we interact with people. For while there is a benefit through God's principle of sowing and reaping, let our only motive be to love God and please Him.

"While crossing over can mean a lot of things to each one of us, here's where it all starts for me: the point where you let go of all doubt and walk fully into God's arms."

Deciding

CROSSING OVER

When I was in grade school, everybody wanted to be a Safety Patrol. You would be the trusted one to make sure it was safe for the other students to cross the street. We had bright white cloth belts to wear that went around our waist and crossed over our chests where we pinned our big silver badge like a Sheriff. Other than getting to clean the chalkboard erasers on the special vacuum cleaner device, that was louder than a jet taking off (the beginning of my tinnitus I'm sure) that was my first recollection of being singled out and having some kind of authority. If we were chosen, we had to learn a special way to roll up the belt as well. Because of the extra piece of strap that crossed our chest, and being nine years old, getting that thing properly rolled up was like figuring out the Rubik's cube.

When I think of crossing over, I think of things like crossing the Atlantic to Europe or going from the US to Canada....gospel music to pop music, earth to heaven, one side of the street to the other. This means something totally different depending on who you're talking to. But ultimately, in one way or another, there's something we all want to know. Is it safe?

Even the Simplest Things Require Thought, a Plan and Action

In most instances crossing over infers something good. A move forward or a move up, something new taking you deeper into your future or to the next destination in your daily journey. Crossing over also requires some decisions before you take that first big step. Even the simple things require thought, a plan and some action. You don't even cross the street without looking both ways, knowing where you are, where you are going and why you are going there.

Sometimes we think of our transition from earth to heaven as the big one; well, it is! This is our promised reward, the completion of a life well lived and God's free gift to all who believe. This comes to us through the great sacrifice Jesus made to reconcile us to the Father. 2 Corinthians 5:4 says, "For while we are in this tent, we groan and are burdened, because we do not wish to be unclothed but to be clothed with our heavenly dwelling, so that what is mortal may be swallowed up by life." (NIV) So, we travel from life to life cradled in the arms of Christ. How beautiful. We also read in 1 Corinthians 2:9 "However, as it is written: 'What no eye has seen, what no ear has heard, and what no human mind has conceived'—the things God has prepared for those who love him." (NIV) Crossing over into that is truly the greatest gift anyone could ever receive.

You Are Either for Him or Against Him

While crossing over can mean a lot of things to each one of us, here's where it all starts for me: the point where you let go of all doubt and walk fully into God's arms. The point where you are either for Him or against Him. It's the moment you realize that if you continue to hide your faith, you are one silent moment away from being ashamed of the One who made you and designed your now and your future. Mark 8:38 says "For whoever is ashamed of Me and My words in this adulterous and sinful generation, of him, the Son of Man also will be ashamed when He comes in the glory of His Father with the holy angels." That scripture and realization changed everything for me. That was the turning point when I crossed over and never looked back.

For myself, and many others I suppose, hanging on to some guilty pleasure was familiar territory. Your guilt was like a dial on a thermostat...the longer you kept your sin alive the hotter the temperature rose. You might release a few vices one by one but that "one thing" would stick around like an unwanted houseguest and set you back time and time again. Proverbs 26:11 says it best: "As a dog returns to its vomit, so fools repeat their folly." (NIV)

Although there is a physical element to our mess, it's really a spiritual battle. An addict's body craves its drug of choice, but the mind always makes the final decision to engage. Ephesians 6:12 puts it this way: "For we do not wrestle against flesh and blood, but against principalities, against powers, against the rulers of the darkness of this age, against spiritual hosts of wickedness in the heavenly places." It's a war of the mind.

One Foot In and One Foot Out

For each of us there needs to come the time when we have had enough; when we are finally done disappointing God by saying yes to only part of Him. One foot in and one foot out. "Lukewarm" as the scriptures say in Revelation 3:16. I'm not a perfect man. Far from it actually. But I have made my choice. I have crossed over, put both feet on the God side. Given all of myself to the one who gave all of Himself for me.

So how about you? Is it your time, is it the day you are finally sick of the guilt meter having the loudest voice in your life? Have you realized at last that a life well lived starts now? Pack your bag, take the good stuff and leave the junk behind. It's safe to cross over. Do it and never look back!

"You don't have to be a diagnosed narcissist to know that it can be a hard fight getting outside of yourself long enough to pay proper attention to the needs of those around you, including the people you love most."

Humility

SELFISH TO SELFLESS

Some journeys are easy. A long trip home to see family. A well needed vacation at the beach. Or a ride to get ice cream on a hot Summer night. Easy because you want to get there. On the other hand, the journey from selfish to selfless is a lot harder because it's about forfeiting your rights. Giving up your "me first" position to a Godly posture of others first. Less of "I" and more of "us." Philippians 2:3 says it best, "Let nothing be done through selfish ambition or conceit, but in lowliness of mind let each esteem others better than himself."

Regarding that big leap, some psychologists might say you can't get there from here, but with God's help I know you can. You don't have to be a diagnosed narcissist to know that it can be a hard fight getting outside of yourself long enough to pay proper attention to the needs of those around you, including the people you love most. The journey from selfish to selfless could be one of the best trips of your life.

Are We There Yet?

It's funny how most of us make our decisions in life based on how we will be affected, but don't often enough take into consideration how our choices in life will affect others.

Am I there yet? Not really, but I think I am getting closer.

As a kid coming from a loving family, I received a lot of affirmation. I felt loved and was always told that I could do anything I put my mind to. That's a good thing and I am forever grateful for it. The problem can be, when a lot of attention is focused your way, you can turn much of your attention toward yourself and become more self-focused as opposed to others-focused.

I can still remember one of my extremely passionate Italian Aunts referring to people being in the "ILM Club" …the I Love Me Club. I was very young and thought that was amusing, but as I got older, I realized she was probably referring to me a bit as well!

Fast Forward

I guess it all started when my uncle bought me a new bowling ball with a turquoise bag that had my name stenciled on the side—I'm not kidding here—in 4" tall letters! I was so embarrassed. I felt like the whole world was watching every time I walked into the bowling alley. Truth is though, it was something that showed I was well loved, and I learned over time that it actually felt pretty good.

Ten years later I'm in a career as a professional musician. There were posters with my name and picture on it advertising the next gig I was playing. Being a musician where eyes and ears are on you a lot, if you're not totally God centered you can think more highly of yourself than you ought, as the Scripture warns. The Apostle Paul says in Romans 12:13 "For by the grace given me I say to every one of you: Do not think of yourself more highly than you ought, but rather think of yourself with sober judgment, in accordance with the faith God has distributed to each of you." (NIV)

Fast Forward Again

Another ten years and I was making records and touring the world, and yes, at least in part, it all seemed to be about me. Even in Christian music I had to wrestle with self-promotion. When you are "the brand," that's what you do. I guess what made me comfortable with it was knowing that it was really all about God. I was just the vehicle. But even with that truth there was still a struggle at times.

There is a point in all our lives where we need to take the focus off ourselves and place it on others. I'm not taking about abandoning your own feelings and desires, but rather getting the whole thing in balance.

Gary Chapman's bestselling book, *The Five Love Languages*, is helpful here. It outlines five ways to express and experience love. It probably comes as no surprise that my main Love Language, like many musicians, is words of affirmation. I can hear my wife loving me with one of her great strengths, which is balance. She'd say something like "I don't have time to stroke you right now, it's a good song, but I have things to do!" I wonder at times if I gravitated towards music because it would speak to my love language and my need for affirmation? I'm not sure but it's an interesting theory.

We Are Programmed to Take Care of Ourselves

Think about it. Everywhere you turn you are inundated with marketing geared to your individual needs and desires. You deserve the best. The best car, home, clothes, creature comforts, etc. We are programmed to take care of ourselves. So, what's wrong with that? Actually, when in balance, nothing. The problem is, we tend to look so inwardly, that we forget about others. Things like serving, reaching out, and making time for thinking and caring for others can easily fall by the wayside.

Throughout the Scriptures we are told to look out-
wardly from ourselves both in thought and action. These
simple, yet powerful verses were written because of the
selfish nature of man and I'm sure the social climate in
the world.

"...love each other, as I have loved you."
John 15:12b

"Be devoted to one another in love.
Honor one another above yourselves."
Romans 12:10 (NIV)

"Therefore, receive one another, just as Christ
also received us, to the glory of God."
Romans 15:7

"So then, my brethren, when you come
together to eat, wait for one another."
Corinthians 11:33 (NASB)

"...through love serve one another."
Galatians 5:13b (NASB)

"Bear one another's burdens"
Galatians 6:2a (NASB)

"Be kind to one another, tender-hearted, forgiving each
other, just as God in Christ also has forgiven you."
Ephesians 4:32 (NASB)

> "...regard one another as
> more important than yourselves;"
> Philippians 2:3b (NASB)

Those are just a few of the "one another" scriptures which speak loudly to selflessness.

The Two Greatest Commandments

There's a beautiful balance within the well-known passage in Mark 12:28-31, "One of the teachers of the law came and heard them debating. Noticing that Jesus had given them a good answer, he asked him, "Of all the commandments, which is the most important?" "The most important one," answered Jesus, "is this: 'Hear, O Israel: The Lord our God, the Lord is one. Love the Lord your God with all your heart and with all your soul and with all your mind and with all your strength.' The second is this: 'Love your neighbor as yourself.' There is no commandment greater than these." (NIV)

Let's love our neighbor. And do everything else the Bible teaches related to loving others. What if we were always concerned about how your choices affect others? What if we were never so inwardly focused that we overlooked the needs and feelings of others?

And notice this gem: love your neighbor as yourself. Not more highly, not less, but "as" yourself. This is part of the balance. There will be times in your life where it may seem that you are putting more emphasis on yourself than you should. Pray, ask God for discernment, ask the Holy Spirit for help. Check yourself with your spouse, pastor or close friend that you trust. Make the adjustment in how you live, so your life reflects these two commandments. What an eternal difference that will make everywhere you are!

Remember, living selflessly doesn't mean not taking care of yourself too. The Bible makes that clear. Seek God so you can have the peace that comes from living in the right balance. Keep your eyes on God as He clears the way along your road, transforming you from selfish to selfless.

"If I am pleasing God, that means my life is in proper alignment. If I am following Godly goals, my family, if they are in right alignment too, will be pleased as well."

Choice

DESIRE V/S RESPONSIBILITY

We all have dreams we want to see fulfilled. I don't think I've ever met a musician that didn't want to be a full-time musician. Most of us love to play so much that we will put just about anything on hold to pursue that dream. That gets more complicated as we become responsible for people other than ourselves. As a single person it's easier to chase after a dream than it is for one who is married and even harder if you're married with kids. The phrase that many of us use is "I've paid my dues." The key here is; did you pay your dues or did your whole family pay them with you?

Over the years I've thought long and hard about the desire that any of us have to take our God given gift and run it up the flagpole. After all, we're not supposed to hide it under a bushel. We are supposed to use our skills for The Lord and cultivate and develop our talents to the point of excellence. Proverbs 18:16a tells us that "A man's gift makes room for him...". (NASB) It will open the way. According to God's Word our gifts WILL come out, they WILL show up. So, what does that mean? To me it means we will either use those gifts within the structure that God sets up for us or use them in a way that feeds our desire but has us unrestrained when faced with a responsibility that should take a higher priority. Feeding our desire and neglecting our responsibility just won't work.

OK, I'll get right to the point. Are you putting your desire to be a full-time musician ahead of your responsibility to provide for your family? I could rephrase that question to address any number of similar situations: The person who is working on his novel but can't pay his mortgage, the executive waiting for a higher paying job while his family is going hungry, the mom taking unpaid acting parts while her kids are waiting at home by the door. These and any number of examples where desire rules over responsibility need to be looked at.

For me, in my early days as a musician, my musical career aspirations led the way and overrode my good judgment more times than not. Was I the guy in the paragraph above? Regretfully, yes.

I remember, in some of my first bands, the pride we had because we were musicians. We put our bands ahead of most things in our life and we were proud of it. As a young father I loved my wife and our kids and would do anything for them. I really thought that. Yet, when I couldn't pay our bills, I kept chasing the dream instead of humbling myself by providing for my family in other ways. I counsel many young (and not so young) musicians, as well as all kinds of people chasing other dreams, that are making the same mistake. And it can, and often does apply, even to those seeking a ministry or missions dream.

There Is a Holy Order to Your Life

Once I came to Christ things started to change. I realized the importance of right alignment in my life and prioritizing things God's way. But the ways we deceive ourselves can be very subtle. Even if my dreams as a musician didn't always come first, that desire for them to BE first contributed to my bad judgment, as I placed my responsibilities as a husband and father on the back burner. If I wanted something badly enough, success, a record deal, being the hot band at all the clubs, whatever, my good sense quickly got clouded.

When I hear of someone with a career dream, prioritizing their life God's way, I have true admiration for them. I celebrate their decisions because I know they are not selfish ones, but rather are choices that put their responsibilities ahead of their own desires: Decisions that speak louder—related to their responsibility to provide—than their desire to chase a dream at all costs.

I've been very blessed to have God's grace on my own life and career. I've managed to work hard and achieve some levels of success in fulfilling some of my own dreams, so I certainly don't want to be the dream buster. But I do want to encourage you to examine your heart regarding this matter.

Bottom line, if you and your spouse are at odds about your music, career of any kind, or ministry, chances are you are not taking care of business at home. If you can't pay your bills, you need to get a job, plain and simple.

Remember, if you are gifted at these disciplines you will never NOT be a musician, artist, actor, author or business executive, etc. "For the gifts and the calling of God are irrevocable" Romans 29:11. And remember Colossians 3:23: "Whatever you do, work at it with all your heart, as working for the Lord." Whatever work we do, when we do it unto the Lord, it's a high calling! And you will feel better about your gifts, both creative and administrative, if you live Biblically, putting first things first. I've counseled many a person to let God redirect some of that passion you have for that dream, into letting Him work deep in your heart, your gifts and every aspect of your life, as you honor Him and your family. That always reaps a good harvest!

Why I spend time telling you how not to blow it, rather than telling you how to succeed at chasing your dream full time, is summed up in the sober truth of this scripture from 1 Timothy 5:8: "But if anyone does not provide for his own, and especially for those of his household, he has denied the faith and is worse than an unbeliever." (NASB). Those are strong words for sure, but true and worth meditating on.

Your Life Should Be a Reflection of Godly Principles

When your life reflects principles that don't line up to God's Word, trouble is on the way. Broken homes, bitter and discouraged people, and gifts that never come to fruition are the result of placing desire over responsibility.

I am a musician. I have felt every tug and pull to nurture my talent to maturity and use what I've been given in a way that brings success. What I've learned, however, is that the more important thing is to use my talent in a way that pleases God. If I am pleasing God, that means my life is in proper alignment. If I am following Godly goals, my family, if they are in right alignment too, will be pleased as well.

So, go after it! Follow your dreams! Work to become exactly who God wants you to be. Use your gifts and talents for Him and, please, prioritize your life God's way so that desire and responsibility don't compete but work hand in hand.

"Love and encouragement go hand in hand
and God knew that we needed them.
The beautiful effects of both start
by giving it freely to others."

Encouragement

WHILE IT'S STILL CALLED TODAY

One Sunday morning in church I saw something beautiful. In observance of Veterans Day our pastor asked all the Vets to stand. Men and women all over the room stood and received our love and appreciation through applause. It was a long lingering moment of gratitude, as it should be. The man in front of me was standing along with the other Veterans. When everyone sat down his wife leaned into him and with a perfect mix of pride and love, mouthed the words "I love you." That did something to me. It reminded me of the great value in passing along words and gestures of love as encouragement to others.

We Are Designed to Receive and Give Love

There are many opportunities to share our feelings of love and admiration with others. God designed us to receive love and to give love. We are made that way. But what we do with it is up to us.

Once again we look at the two greatest commandments. They both contain the word love. "Teacher, which is the greatest commandment in the law?" Jesus said to him, 'You shall LOVE the Lord your God with all your heart, with all your soul, and with all your mind.' This is the first and greatest commandment. And the second is like it: 'You shall LOVE your neighbor as yourself'" Matthew 22:36-39

Love God and love your neighbor. Again, in John 15:17 are we reminded of this commandment. "These things I command you, that you love one another." For some it's a natural response to the gratitude we have in our hearts. Yet for others, love is hard to muster up for a number of reasons.

Some, out of fear, harbor these feelings until they are either forgotten or their impact is diluted by the passing of time. Those expressions of love and encouragement that God ordained by the prompting of the Holy Spirit are overlooked, then spiral down into the keyless vault of lost opportunities. Others blame God for every bad thing that happens. So, loving Him is governed by the lie that evil is His fault. Some, on the other hand, have no problem loving God but loving people is where they struggle. If you have been hurt over and over again, your guard is up, and you put everyone in the same category...not safe, not worthy to be loved.

And let's realize too, that just as we are commanded to love, we are commanded to encourage one another. Hebrews 3:13 says; "But encourage one another daily, as long as it is called 'Today,' so that none of you may be hardened by sin's deceitfulness." (NIV) And again, in 1 Thessalonians 5:11, "Therefore encourage one another and build each other up, just as in fact you are doing." (NIV)

Love and encouragement go hand in hand and God knew that we needed them. The beautiful effects of both start by giving it freely to others. The Word of God also says we will reap what we sow. Through that promise, then encouragers will receive encouragement.

Nurture the Gifts of Others

Many young children start their lives with natural gifts and abilities. These gifts and abilities start to manifest at a very early age. If they are nurtured, celebrated and encouraged these young ones will mature and make us all better by sharing what they have been given to an eagerly waiting world.

On the other hand, if our best intentions of helping our kids manifests itself as criticism, then that criticism may outweigh or overpower our praise. We have put a ball and chain on their joyful motivation to fully develop their gifts. Please, let's remember the words of Hebrews 3:13. Think before you speak, especially if the words that are about to be uttered don't reflect the commandments to love and encourage.

I can remember on many occasions watching some young person doing something, maybe even a very simple task, exercising a God given gift or talent. The moment I spoke encouragement into what they were doing, their pace picked up a bit. They stood up a little straighter and a smile came on their faces. No matter what age, we are all built for encouragement, and when it's given, we are better for it. And, if words of encouragement are the recipient's emotional "love language" they are exponentially better. We also have to trust that even people who don't seem to respond the way we would hope, are moved as well.

From God to Us, from Us to Others

While I'm grateful to have received love and encouragement over the years, I can remember times when something I worked very hard at went overlooked. It was in those instances I looked immediately to God. Even in my early years, when it was more instinct than relationship, I truly felt His pleasure. Let's remember that our motive should always be to serve God and others. But, as I mentioned earlier, there is a reward that comes back to us by His design.

Through all of this we must remember that it's hard to give something away that you don't possess yourself. Love and encouragement are best delivered to others if we first have received plenty of it. I pray that each of you have received loads of both throughout your lifetime. If you haven't, Jesus has you well covered! He loves you, unconditionally! Continue to look to Him throughout each day to reinforce who He says you are, and how wonderfully unique you have been made.

There is much in life that comes directly from God for our instruction and growth. There is also great value in observing others sharing Godly values to mankind through purposeful acts of kindness, love and encouragement. As we go through life, let's be doers of the Word (James 1:22). Let's be observers with a purpose: to seek out opportunities to freely give encouragement and love, while it's still called "today"!

"It's amazing to me how many of us are well equipped yet we listen to the voice of the enemy and let his lies undermine the plans that God has for us."

Balance

WHERE'S ONE?

For musicians, we've been there so many times…trying to discover where the first beat of the measure is. It might happen in the beginning of us playing a song together or anywhere during. Sometimes you figure it out in the first few bars but sometimes the only way out is looking at the drummer mouthing the words "where's one?". The real nightmare is when the drummer looks back at you, shakes his head and shrugs. Believe me, every performing musician has experienced that a few times!

In recordings it's artfully calculated. The guitar player or keyboard player might start a groove but it's turned around, meaning the drummer may be partially in but with no backbeat. In pop music the backbeat is when the drummer hits his snare drum on beats two and four of each measure. Also, the other musicians could be playing something a bit odd and not settled into the solid groove. When it finally kicks in properly it's very cool and everything feels right again. You can breathe, you smile and everything's good.

It's similar in live situations. Even though it might be planned you may have gotten distracted just enough to be momentarily lost. Any player could be the culprit. I work a lot with drummers who will intentionally turn the beat around for eight bars, maybe longer, but then land on the one with authority and confidence. Those times are fun because the band just stays the course until the backbeat returns. Those interesting musical moments can remain solid while they are in process or if not properly executed feel like the times when a glass falls out of the cupboard and is precariously juggled from hand to hand until it is either safely caught or smashes to pieces on the floor.

Another amazing thing is when the singer enters the song turned around and instead of correcting the problem, the band refuses to adjust to him or her. It's as if the band is saying, "you're wrong and were not going to help you!" Believe me that happens. Our job, as musicians, is to help each other out and not to try and prove how smart we think we are. The smartest move is everyone working together to make it wonderful.

The parallel in life are those days when you feel off balance...off your game. Some days I get up and everything just flows but other times it all feels left footed. I just float, wanting so much to be grounded and steady. I want to settle into the groove of the day, but I just can't pull it into my sights. The good news is, usually, when you're off balance, the only one who knows it is you. That's the bad news too though. Because no one knows, you are on your own.

In both cases, in music and in life, the natural reaction is to act like everything's just perfect, move to the music, think on your feet and hope for the best. If we trust God, we know that "...All things work together for good..." Romans 8:28a. That's the happy ending but it can be a bit daunting when you're in the middle of it.

When you're out of sync the first thing you need to do it MAKE SURE YOU'RE THINKING RIGHT. If you are starting to get fearful pray God's word over yourself. 2 Timothy 1:7 says; "For God has not given us a spirit of fear, but of power and of love and of a sound mind." The minute thoughts that are contrary to God's word and His promises for us enter our mind get in the habit of immediately taking them captive. 2 Corinthians 10:5 says; "casting down arguments and every high thing that exalts itself against the knowledge of God, bringing every thought into captivity to the obedience of Christ."

Next you need to PAUSE BRIEFLY. Take a moment or two or whatever you need to just wait and then resume your pace with confidence. Truth is, your feeling of being off balance is happening within you. As far as everyone else is concerned nothing has changed. Let that reality become your reality as you steady yourself forward.

Lastly you need to be comfortable with the fact that EVERY DAY IS DIFFERENT. If you think back even a short time you will agree. It's an adventure but always one with great hope and the promises of God to light our way. It's amazing to me how many of us are well equipped yet we listen to the voice of the enemy and let his lies undermine the plans that God has for us. Fear, unbelief, lack of confidence, etc. You need to know that God is for you and made you in His image to succeed. Anything else is a lie and you need to dismantle those thoughts quickly.

So, what do you do when you're off balance, when you can't find "one"? Stay close to God and each other, be anxious for nothing, take every thought captive to the obedience of Christ, move to the music. And with Godly confidence, dance your dance of life.

"The goal is to hear from God, live well and

in His will and purpose for our lives."

Completion

TWENTY-FIVE

IT'S ALL IN THE HEARING

Among the many happy things in my life are my in-ear monitors. Think of tiny headphones that are perfectly molded to fit snuggly inside your ears. They help me actually hear what is going on while performing, which as you can imagine, is really important for a musician. Other than playing at church with a personal monitor mixer and in-ear monitors, I have always been a wedge guy (those big speakers they put in the floor in front of musicians when they are on stage, so the band's mix blasts back at them). Actually, in the early years none of us used monitors of any kind. We just sang as loud as we could and hoped for the best!

Of late, I'm not hoping for the best, I have the best. From the first time I inserted my in-ear monitors and locked them in place, I was in a whole new world. I was like a kid with my first bike. I didn't know I could have such incredible isolation and full spectrum sound.

When You Hear Well You Play Well

You can't play well with other people unless you can hear them. On stage, where the volume can get out of hand, you may find yourself looking at the drummer's kick pedal just to be sure you are in the groove. Looking helps, but hearing is essential. When a singer sings part of the verse, chorus, or bridge lyric to cue the band, you need to hear that cue to be able to go there. Although we follow charts, we want to accommodate freedom as well. And, as most musicians know, playing in the moment is where the wonderful is.

Another area critical to hearing is knowing when to lay back and when to step out. When you are hearing the whole band, you can get into the zone easier, making the way for great playing and not stepping on your band in the process. Most train wrecks happen when musicians can't hear well. Add to that the mental distraction that comes from it taking you totally out of the band and into a very uncomfortable place.

Being completely honest I have to say that there is a unique joy that comes from wonderfully mixed wedges as opposed to in-ear monitors. There's nothing like hearing the overall sound from the room. But, as wonderful as it can be, it's also dependent on many factors, most of which are out of your control.

When You Hear Well You Live Well

In Isaiah 55:3 we read "Incline your ear, and come to Me. Hear, and your soul shall live; and I will make an everlasting covenant with you—The sure mercies of David."

Just as we can get distracted when we play by not hearing well, in life, not hearing well along with the worries of the moment, insecurity, and the like can also distract us. The goal is to hear from God, live well and in His will and purpose for our lives. Hearing God is the first step to that. The hope is that hearing leads to understanding then understanding to obedience. "Hear and your soul shall live." We have to live to experience life the way God intended it.

There's another gem in that verse. What are "The sure mercies of David" that are promised to us in Isaiah 55:3 when we Incline our ear and hear? These mercies, part of the everlasting covenant, are eternally faithful loving-kindnesses. All this from hearing! It's foundational; it's the beginning step to so many good things. Things that are essential for living both naturally and spiritually.

When You Hear Well You Finish Well

Starting is only the beginning. How many unfinished projects do you have going on? Whether it's a song, a task around the house, a job or ministry responsibility or the BIG finish of life, hearing will help you complete well the things that you start.

And to start, you need faith. Romans 10:17 says "So then faith comes by HEARING, and hearing by the word of God." You have to believe in your heart that you can do it, whatever the "it" is. Can you do it? Philippians 4:13 says yes! "I can do ALL THINGS through Christ that strengthens me." Remember...faith to believe starts with hearing.

Next you need to be confident that if you do your part God will do His. In Philippians 1:6b we read "He who has begun a good work in you will complete it until the day of Jesus Christ." Again, we see that the beginning, hearing God's word, leads to believing and believing leads to completion.

There have always been people in my life that I have observed up close or from a distance that I admired; men, women, people from all walks of life and with various skills. No one was alike but they all had this in common: the Jesus factor. The word says that we will know them by their fruit, and what good fruit they all had. While we should live our lives to be more like Christ, I love how we are given Godly examples along the way to watch closely and be inspired by.

150

My prayer for each of you and myself is that by God's grace and by hearing and believing we will all live our lives displaying the qualities that speak to finishing well. Whether it's that small but important task at hand or the grand finale of life on this earth, let's be hearers and doers. When we are finally swallowed by eternal life, let's enter heaven as those who heard well to finish well, living every day to its ordained completion in Christ.

"From God to each of us comes discernment and the ability to gather our views, likes and dislikes and represent or resemble the things that move us and that we believe in."

Discernment

A MATTER OF TASTE

Personal taste encompasses many things. Yet it's often as simple as what kind of foods are our favorites, what style clothes we gravitate to, or "I love charcoal gray." Likes and dislikes sum this up pretty accurately.

A bit of emotion comes into play for decisions on some matters of taste. But way more emotion, and closer to the surface, is present when we move beyond taste to what we personally think is cool or hip, and how deeply that matters to us. You like chicken I like fish, OK, great! No fight in that. But try to convince someone that your favorite band, for example, is better than theirs and you may have a battle on your hands!

If you say something is hip, there's an assumption, when you use that word, that you may be more of an authority on the subject. The "Hipster" many times is on thin ice in social circles unless those groups of people are all kindred in their taste.

#2 Now, the Word of God and its values are absolute. All of life is subject to Jesus as Lord. And much of life is flavored with personal taste and interpretation too, as long as it falls in line with Biblical truth. Beauty is in the eye of the beholder, and similarly our likes and dislikes vary from person to person. Yes, we have our tribes and like-minded circles of friends, but, the final thumbs up on coolness or what is truly hip is an individual choice.

"Fearfully and wonderfully made" is how the Scripture describes us in Psalm 139:14. And that quickly comes to mind when I think about all this. Everyone is an individual, designed by God, who is the original Creative Person. The Author and Dispatcher of everything that makes us who we are. Every nuance, like, dislike, and our opinion on beauty comes from the hand of God, starting at our creation and developing throughout our life experience. To be clear, I am not saying that likes and dislikes that don't line up to godliness come from God. Just think of Philippians 4:8: "Finally, brethren, whatever is true, whatever is honorable, whatever is right, whatever is pure, whatever is lovely, whatever is of good repute, if there is any excellence and if anything worthy of praise, dwell on these things (NASB)."

Our Individual Taste Is a Unique Gift

But what is hip? For many of us, this isn't a question, it's one of Tower of Power's greatest hit songs. Who could forget that incredible bass line that Francis "Rocco" Prestia recorded? It was like a Tommy Gun riveting us to the wall of bass envy. Possibly the most memorable sixteenth note staccato bass track of all time. For sure that song was hip.

The Urban Dictionary defines hip as "cooler than cool, the pinnacle of what is "it." Beyond all trends and conventional coolness." Merriam-Webster says, "having or showing awareness of or involvement in the newest developments or styles." To some this second definition is a lot less hip than the first. People can be all over the map, even when it comes to definitions!

But there are two important things to remember here. First, we need to be thankful that God made us all with our own personal opinion. Everything isn't supposed to look the same to everybody. Things look as they do based on our interpretation, not someone else's. Likes and dislikes may not be different shades of grey, but the whole color palette! Our individual taste is a gift and the outcome of everything working in our lives: God's Word, our DNA, environment, the leanings of our unique friends and an inner spiritual sense that God bestows on every believer who calls Him Lord.

Next, we need to always remember that taste is OUR opinion. Possibly the best for us, but certainly not for all. Ephesians 4:32a tells us to "Be kind to one another, tender hearted..." (NASB). One characteristic of kindness is respecting the opinions of others and doing it sincerely. Not with a roll of the eyes or a smirk that suggests your opinion is better than theirs. Rather, with a sincere kind heart that realizes they too have a right to their opinion, and it may be as good as yours. Actually, based on the subject matter and the experience of the one who delivers the opinion, it may be even better. But wait, can an opinion really be better? Not really because it's an opinion not fact. It may be better to the person who has it but totally off the wall to someone else.

Looking back at some of my friends I can easily recall different personalities that either held on to every opinion of theirs like gospel or held on loosely knowing that there were many valid opinions on the subject. Another thing worth mentioning is that our taste is subjective. Fact is not.

Comfortable in Your Own Skin

Have you ever noticed that someone's hipness, if that's even a word, is truly based on their own opinion of what's cool? Of course, what one person thinks is cool, more often than not started in someone else's mind. Then it, through their actions, style, dress, composition or some other viewable or listenable medium, was delivered to you. That's especially true when someone lives within the mainstream. Someone who is dialed in to pop culture.

So how about those who live outside of the mainstream? I can remember an artist who walked around with one pant leg rolled up to his knee. Just one. He owned that style, believed in it and wore it with confidence. I kept waiting to see it catch on, even a bit, but it never seemed to, at least I didn't see it. It was just his style, an individual fashion statement that he was comfortable with. Hip? Cool? Maybe. Maybe just to him. Yet he owned it with no apology.

On the other hand, somebody—usually very well known—starts a trend. And being comfortable in their own skin they own it the same as the pant leg fellow. But this time it takes off. Go figure. Maybe it's because of their broader reach. Who knows?

Hey, at the end of the day that's all up to you. It's about your own thoughts, ideas and interpretations. From God to each of us comes discernment and the ability to gather our views, likes and dislikes and represent or resemble the things that move us and that we believe in. So, read it, watch it, listen to it, wear it, write it, play it, share it, ride it, drive it, love it! Your own unique Hipapalooza happening in and through you and passed along to those in your world.

That killer song, that beautiful car, that lovely dress. That amazing movie, breathtaking landscape, inspiring book. That observed or self-initiated act of kindness. All bring us back to this "...whatever is pure, whatever is lovely, whatever is of good repute, if there is any excellence and if anything worthy of praise, dwell on these things" (Philippians 4:8 NASB).

So, what's really important here? Within Biblical, Godly bounds, be your own person. Latch on to things you like no matter what the popular opinion is. Be unique and mean it! And at the same time let respect for others rule. Beauty is all around us, but at the end of the day how we see it is often a just matter of taste.

"From the simplest things to navigating

your career, ministry or relationships,

without good discernment, you could miss

a golden opportunity or at worst be like a bull

in the proverbial china shop."

Discernment

TWENTY-SEVEN

INTERPRETATION IS EVERYTHING

Being able to rightly interpret every encounter or situation you find yourself in, is always your starting point to a best outcome. From the simplest things to navigating your career, ministry or relationships, without good discernment, you could miss a golden opportunity or at worst be like a bull in the proverbial china shop.

Let's use the musician as an example. Assuming he or she knows their way around their instrument, has developed their listening skills and is pretty much proficient at playing with a group, interpretation can be the difference between nailing it or just getting by.

Let's say the band is playing a funk tune. The reality is, everyone interprets in his or her own unique way. We are talking about players with a certain level of experience. Most everyone can "do the job" but the player who gets talked up and called back for another live gig or recording session is the one whose interpretation lifts their part above the rest and puts a premium on their value. Many musicians have been there. The new guy comes in and within several bars everybody is blown away. In this case he has brought something new to the piece, partially by discerning who he's playing with, and it encourages everyone in the band to dig a little deeper and play with more passion.

One personal example I could give is a time when we were working up a new tune that was okay but wasn't great. It was mid-tempo and just didn't seem to get off the ground. As I listened, I thought I would change up the bass part and play it reggae. Honestly, I think I was getting bored and having no fun at all, so maybe it was a happy accident. Yet one by one the band abandoned their original parts and started playing reggae as well. Each one developed the perfect part for the tune based on their interpretive skills. We never looked back. That was exactly what was needed to take the song from average to very cool. This same thing has happened over the years with various players leading the way. Interpreting their part not just to fit the song, but actually enhance it, causing a chain reaction within the band. On the contrary, if I had taken an obstinate posture and stuck with a bass part that didn't work best, it could've been a disaster. Not only for the tune but for future callbacks.

No matter what your career, ministry or gifting is, interpreting your surroundings, including the people you are working with and the new idea on the table is critical. I am sharing my thoughts related to music because that's where I have spent much of my time. I am stating the obvious here—which is also one of my gifts by the way—but the business person, athlete, graphic designer, school teacher, CPA, etc. interpret their world daily as well. The ones who do it best are the ones who are thoroughly dialed in, and through that they become experts at it.

So How Do We Get There?

Being excellent at interpretation comes with a price. You have to want it badly. This can't be something low on the priority list. Beneath God, spouse & family it must be at or very close to the top. For us musicians, when we were younger players, we would spend hours listening to the greats. We would play our gig for 4 hours, eat (very important), then sit in the car and listen to some distant all-night radio station that played our favorite jazz for hours more. We would implement what we learned the next night on the bandstand and over time what we learned from others, morphed into licks, feel and technique that became our own. That's how it happens...it's the musical or career food chain...we get from someone, who got from someone, who got from someone and on and on and on.

Genetics, Environment & Hard Work

Let's start at the beginning. Genetics, what you are born with will many times move you toward your career or calling. You've heard the expression "the fruit doesn't fall far from the tree." If your parents or someone in your genetic up-line are musical, business minded, athletic, etc. there's a good chance you will be too. Although, by itself, that may not be enough, it's a great start!

Next, what you grow up around, your environment, will also play a critical role in how you look at and participate in the things you lean toward. Whatever skills were regularly active in your home would be the things you would most likely gravitate towards. As you observed your parents or siblings participating you would most likely jump in too and be encouraged to do so. One of the best examples I could give, besides music, is sports. For kids that grow up in homes where sports are a daily part of life, you too will be playing sports. Again, environment plays a critical role in the initial development of your skills.

Now, the toughest part requiring the most discipline is hard work. This is the amount of time you study and practice to hone your craft. For the musician we call it "wood-shedding." I would imagine that came from being asked to take your music outside in the shed where the volume wouldn't bother anyone. There is no getting around this one. People who are great, not just good, build on, not squander, what they have been given through genetics and environment alone. They enhance their foundation to bring their skill to perfection by working hard. Genetics, environment and hard work. The first two are a gift. The last one is a commitment.

Interpretation in Life

Interpretation is critical for all of us, vital in our everyday lives. As you navigate relationships, grow in God's Word and discern all that life brings, you need to be tightly focused. Be sensitive and able to think on your feet as you interpret every situation that you are faced with. Also, if you interpret your skills, ministry and career well, but can't understand your wife, husband, kids or friends, you need to ask God to help you grow in this area and reprioritize your life.

God has generously given all sorts of different gifts and talents to each of us. So, remember…to whom much is given, much is required. That's you! Greatness is my prayer for each of us; in our professional and ministerial lives, in relationships, and most of all in Christ.

"Knowing where your gifts and talents come from and being humbly grateful to the Giver keeps us balanced in a Godly way."

Pride

TWENTY-EIGHT

WATCH YOUR STEP

Sometimes our biggest mistakes follow our biggest victories. I have always been acutely aware of the well-known and often quoted scripture, "Pride goes before destruction and a haughty spirit before a fall" (Proverbs 16:18).

This has played out many times in my life and sometimes in this setting: I am in church on the stage (or the platform as we sometimes refer to it), with the worship team and I am giving God all I have. Playing brave and bold as I return the talent He gave me, in sincere worship to Him. It goes from earth to heaven delivered in a flurry of appropriately placed notes, released into the air with style and verve. Then, just when I think I've played something earth shatteringly great that has surely filled people's worship with awe and wonder (a gross exaggeration, but continuing with the point), I make a HUGE mistake. Not just a tiny one, but one that will be remembered—or so I think—for years to come. The "clam" that was heard around the world.

Wow! I felt a little too good about myself and once again I am reminded of that timeless truth in Proverbs.

Now don't misunderstand, we musicians work very hard at getting out of the way, so people can worship God without distraction. But the reality that there are hundreds of people in front of us can sometimes pull us into performance mode. We need to keep God's purpose for us being there, to point people to Him, always firmly in mind.

When you do something that may truly be good, even great, the tendency is to let pride well up in you as you bask in the afterglow of your perceived brilliance. At that moment the band (if you are a musician), or your coworkers (no matter what your vocation), continue forward needing 100% of you. But a critical chunk of your needed focus is still distracted by your moment of glory. Oh, King Solomon, author and compiler of Proverbs, was surely very wise and most likely realized this truth in his own life as well as the lives of others in his community.

There's a very thin line between pride and Godly confidence. So thin that you could easily vacillate back and forth even in a matter of seconds. Godly confidence is when we realize what God has given us and we don't shrink back from fully using it. Exodus 35:31 says "and he has filled him with the Spirit of God, with wisdom, with understanding, with knowledge and with all kinds of skills" (NIV). That's not prideful or arrogant, its honoring God and blessing others with the gifts and talents we have received from Him. Pride is believing it's all about you. Romans 12:3 says this "For through the grace given to me I say to everyone among you not to think more highly of himself than he ought to think; but to think so as to have sound judgment, as God has allotted to each a measure of faith (NASB)." Our faith keeps us grounded in the truth.

This struggle can occur in every area of life. From the blue-ribbon baker at the State Fair to the powerful CEO running a multinational corporation. Knowing where your gifts and talents come from and being humbly grateful to the Giver keeps us balanced in a Godly way. Whatever you are made for and wherever God has you use these gifts and talents, use them to their fullest measure. Use them appropriately, with discernment and care as you daily walk out your calling.

Philippians 4:13 says "I can do all things through Christ who strengthens me." The "I" in this scripture is underscored with God's power. Actually, it only works with His power. It's His strength working in and through us and it's because of that we can do ALL things. When you know it's God who gives you your gifts and talents you can be sure of these words from the Apostle Paul, "For I am confident of this very thing, that He who began a good work in you will perfect it until the day of Christ Jesus" (Philippians 1:6 NASB).

Some people can take things to the extreme. On the side of pride, well, you've seen these people. They strut around with an air of arrogance giving off an unbecoming odor that can't be missed. And equally sad are the folks on the other end of this, living in fear and hiding what they have been given. But the Bible says "You are the light of the world. A city set on a hill cannot be hidden; nor does anyone light a lamp and put it under a basket, but on the lampstand, and it gives light to all who are in the house. Let your light shine before men in such a way that they may see your good works and glorify your Father who is in heaven" (Matthew 5:14-16 NASB).

You can be sure of this: every good thing God gives you should be used to its fullest measure. And God will give you the wisdom to do that in ways that are healthy and best for the Kingdom, for yourself and for others. Don't go through life hunched over in a shadow. Stand up straight and press ahead knowing that He's got you and has equipped you to succeed. Watch your step when it comes to pride. Move ahead with Godly confidence and leave a legacy that will encourage others for generations to come!

"There are some things we let go of forever
and some for a season. Either way
when we let God direct our decisions,
we are always richer for it."

Responsibility

STUFF I GOT RID OF

A while ago, I was at the North American Music Mer-
chandisers show (NAMM). It's a big, fun tradeshow
event, the world's largest, for the music products industry. I was talking about an old Framus Star bass guitar I
sold in the sixties for probably $100.00. Surely that same
instrument would be worth way more today. I was with
my good friend Tom Lane at the time and he used the
expression "stuff we got rid of." We all have a list and as I
began thinking through on mine, I discovered something
way deeper.

There was the '64 Fender Bassman amp, the red
and black Ampeg scroll top bass with the f-holes, the

several early '70's Rickenbacker basses; the black one, the electric blue one, the blond one, all with that beautiful piping inlaid around the body. The Acoustic 360 bass amp, the Heil Talk Box, and on and on goes the list. In every case I had a good reason to sell something. And in every case, I now look back with regret, or, let's just say light regret.

It was the same with my motorcycles; the BSA 441 Victor, The Triumph Trophy, the 1940 Harley Knuckle-head that my friend John Amos chopped for me over a year of anxious anticipation; Springer front end 14 inches over stock, raked an inch and a half, many custom parts, skillfully airbrushed and sold for a fraction of what it would be worth today. My investment in that bike back then was probably $1,500.

Then came September 6, 1970. Our first daughter, Niki Marie, was born. It was time to sell that Harley. And it was one of the best decisions I've made. Finally, that bike was something I got rid of with no regret, actually with great joy. A decision made for my family. A small personal sacrifice that set me on a new course. When the timing is right, some stuff you get rid of truly makes you better. That was the beginning of a new thinking pattern that I am still working on today, refining it year by year with God's help.

1 Corinthians 13:11 says: "When I was a child, I spoke as a child, I understood as a child, I thought as a child; but when I became a man, I put away childish

things." Some things aren't necessarily childish in and of themselves, but they can become childish based on the circumstances surrounding them. I had cool "stuff," yet we were struggling to buy diapers and pay the rent. Not good.

Circumstances Point to a Greater Need

Although my becoming a man was gradual, and certainly continues, I believe I turned a corner that day. I realized my circumstances pointed to a greater need. Not just for my family but for me. I was beginning to get outside of myself. I was making decisions based on the wellbeing of others, which I discovered actually led to my own wellbeing. I would come to realize that the real personal sacrifice, which could lead to deep regret later in life, is neglecting responsibilities that hold a higher value than things I could certainly live without.

We all have a moment, actually many, when the light goes on and the higher purpose of our existence and responsibility becomes illuminated enough that change happens. It starts as a thought, moves into a decision and ends with a deep satisfying exhale.

There are some things we let go of forever and some for a season. Either way when we let God direct our decisions, we are always richer for it. As it turns out, 40 years after I sold my last motorcycle, with Diana's strong and convincing encouragement, I got another one. This time, with my priorities in order, there was no hesitation or regret.

Old Regrets

So, let's talk about old regrets. I have load of them. And, each one boldly came into existence as the result of a bad decision. None accidental, all deliberately made without restraint. God's word tells us in Proverbs 29:18 "Where there is no revelation, people cast off restraint; but blessed is the one who heeds wisdom's instruction." (NIV)

There comes a point in most of our lives where "wisdom's instruction" gets our attention. It makes us stand up straight and listen. Stop what we are doing, what we are thinking, and contemplate the consequences and the impact our actions will have on others and certainly on us. At best the repercussions of our bad decisions will fade over time. But they most likely stick around for a lifetime like a bad smell that stops you in your tracks just when you almost forgot that foolish thing ever happened.

Just so you know, I don't live there; in that regretful place that keeps you focused on the missteps you've been forgiven for. In that dark depressing introspective hole that keeps you down low, on the bottom. That place that arrests your progress and keeps you from realizing what the rest of life might look like and what your place in it is meant to be.

When you receive enough revelation from the lives of others and directly from God you need to take that gift and move forward. Philippians 3:12-14 declares "Not that I have already obtained all this, or have already

176

arrived at my goal, but I press on to take hold of that for which Christ Jesus took hold of me. Brothers and sisters, I do not consider myself yet to have taken hold of it. But one thing I do: Forgetting what is behind and straining toward what is ahead, I press on toward the goal to win the prize for which God has called me heavenward in Christ Jesus." (NIV)

So, let's sum it all up: Know that everything in your life has purpose, hang on to what's good, get rid of what isn't and look forward to the richness of what God has for you, and for others, through your example!

"Although this human dismantling is something we will all face, I was really thinking of focusing mostly on something totally different. A different dismantling. One that makes you better and actually takes you up, not down and out."

Transformation

THE DISMANTLING OF JOHN DOE

Getting older is interesting. Changes that you never expected to happen start to bloom like weeds in a garden. Things you never thought much about become the topic of normal conversation. Do you remember when your older relatives mostly chatted about their medical procedures? Whether their plumbing worked properly after their second cup of morning coffee? We didn't really relate...until we did!

Depending on your age, this is one topic that may not seem to connect now but tuck this chapter away because you will totally identify one day down the road. There's truth here that if you get now, you'll be way better off later, for yourself and for others.

As of this writing I am starting my 8th decade. It's been a cake walk up until now. Eat well, exercise, avoid stress, count your blessings, etc. Now I can't even squat down without wondering how I'm going to get back up. Sometimes I shampoo, what little hair I have, twice because I forgot I did it the first time. My active mind doesn't allow me to focus on just one thing. My TPM (thoughts per minute) number is out of control! I am an efficiency expert's nightmare.

How about this...I am walking out of the house feeling my pockets for my cell phone only to realize that I am talking on it. Or, I am unpacking my suitcase one morning after returning from a trip and didn't see my belt. I was sure I left it in the hotel room until I realized, way later in the day, it was on my pants. Then, I was playing with my grandkids when they grabbed onto my belt, one on the front and one on the back, and started to swing between my legs. I thought I would just walk them around the house until they got tired, but they brought me down in less than a minute like a wounded gazelle. I couldn't stop laughing, but realized I was coming apart!

A Dismantling That Takes You Up Not Down

Although this human dismantling is something we will all face, I was really thinking of focusing mostly on something totally different. A different dismantling. One that makes you better and actually takes you up, not down and out.

As our lives are assembled through the years, especially the early ones, we bolt on many thoughts, habits and patterns that shape who we are. These character traits are the result of our DNA and even more our experiences with life and those we walk through life with. Good habits and bad ones, that we have welcomed in, attach themselves to us. They cure and season over the years until they become us; who we are, how we think and act.

"This is just who I am," "take it or leave it," "if you don't like it don't look" are just a few of the quips some of us may have used to justify our actions and defend our position. Modeling bad behavior got us there and pride keeps us there. If you ask me it's all just a front to keep us from taking the risk of letting people in and just being normal.

The question I ask myself and would ask you too is: What is the foundation we are standing on? What makes up who we are? Is it a conglomeration of this and that? Things we learned here and there? Just a random selection of bits of life? Or something that we have really thought about based on the truth of who God says we are and guidelines that line up to His word. Without question we do learn from others through our daily observation of life around us. The things we let into the fabric of our being, however, need to be filled with goodness and truth. They need to be the things that will build us and others up by our example.

It's like a personal mission statement. Everything you do should line up to those guiding words. I exist to, I will live my life by, etc. Of course, life isn't just a guide-line driven journey. It's a beautiful mix of absolutes for-mulated over time and spontaneous decisions decided upon in that unique moment. The key here is that your spontaneous decisions have to rest on some of the boundaries you have already set in place through your years of trial and error and hearing from God. As you continue to dismantle bad thinking you adapt good think-ing into your own functional day to day living.

Behavior Worth Learning

There can be something very sweet about discovery when you totally relate to something and want to emulate that behavior. It could be as simple as a business man on a plane giving up his aisle seat for a middle seat so a family can sit together. Or, observing somebody encour-aging and building up someone who really needed it. Things as basic as that can be game changers in the lives of others. When something thoughtful is done for people with entitlement issues, their reaction may be muted, but for most it's a big deal. Especially for the folks that haven't been treated well earlier in life or even moments before.

2 Corinthians 5:20a says "We are therefore Christ's ambassadors, as though God were making his appeal through us." (NIV) If we want to make a deposit in the lives of others, effect culture as Christ's ambassadors, we need to clean house and replace bad thinking and habits with good ones.

So, I'll leave you with two questions. What are the learned behaviors in your life that need to be dismantled? And, what new things have you learned that need to become part of who you are? Why don't you take a minute now and pray and think about that… it can change everything.

"There is an eternal prize for finishing well.

Not a prize from competing against others

but a prize based on what we have been given

and what we have chosen to do with it."

Perseverance

FINISH WELL
ONE DAY AT A TIME

"Therefore, since we are surrounded by such a great cloud of witnesses, let us throw off everything that hinders and the sin that so easily entangles. And let us run with perseverance the race marked out for us," (Hebrews 12:1 NIV)

Throughout my lifetime I have heard people use the expression "finish well." Mostly it has been in reference to the final finish, the end of one's life. I can remember doing a concert for a church when I was in my mid-forties.

When I finished what seemed to be a successful night, both musically and at the altar, the pastor's wife came up to me, looked me square in the eyes and said, "Rick, you are going to finish well." I was both encouraged and petrified! I was already dealing with middle age: Do I still have value? Am I still effective? And, what happened to my hair!? It almost seemed like a prophetic utterance of my impending demise.

It probably took months to shake off what I should have known in the first place: finishing well is a daily hope. The future reward for finishing every day well is the cumulative effect of all those days lived for Christ. It all adds up, one day at a time, to the grand finale. The final finish, hearing the Master say, "Well done good and faithful servant!" (Matthew 25:23)

You Are Not Competing Against Others

"Do you not know that those who run in a race all run, but one receives the prize? Run in such a way that you may obtain it." 1 Corinthians 9:24

There is an eternal prize for finishing well. Not a prize from competing against others but a prize based on what we have been given and what we have chosen to do with it. It's our race, and although others are in the race, its ultimately between us and God. We've all heard the term "personal best" and the U.S. Army slogan, "Be All That You Can Be." Whether it's our gifts and talents, or the people in our lives or in our path; what we do with these things, as we continue to nurture and develop them, is the true measure of who we are. To me, however, it can be the "others" in our personal race, which are the distractions that can slow us down. Whether it's other people or other things, let's be careful to keep our eyes on Him and not let distractions take us off course. Remember, it's your race designed by God. Let's love others along the way but keep your priorities in proper alignment. By God's power working in and through us, we need to choose to persevere and come out not only ahead, but with God's great approval.

Here's some good news of the gospel. We are loved by God unconditionally, based on what Christ has done for us. There's nothing we can do to make God love us more than He already does! Yet because of that very fact, we should steward what we have been given and take our calling and mission very seriously. God's love for us should help us want to please Him the way a child loves their precious father. We have been given a gift, the free gift of salvation. That's where our earthly journey will end but this incredible gift is just the beginning of our new life here.

I'm always reminded that faith is the fuel for the good works we will do along the way. God's Word says that "faith without works is dead" James 2:26b. Our personal faith is completed when we transition to heaven, but we can leave a legacy behind to encourage others in their journey.

We Are All Moving Toward Legacy

Legacy is something we receive from an ancestor, predecessor or someone from the past. Most of us recognize that meaning of legacy but rarely think about it when we are young. It's only when we become more concerned with doing things that are significant and that have lasting impact, does legacy move from a distant thought to something regularly on our minds. While we as believers are promised eternity, we only have our appointed time here on earth. The Word compares our life to a vapor, here then gone, (James 4:14). Scriptures like these have more meaning as life progresses. Remember when you were a kid and fifty seemed unfathomably old. Well, there will come a day for many of us when we are decades beyond that. Some will wish they could go back in time while others will still feel like, and have the ambition of, a thirty-year-old. May the latter be true for us, because of our living Christ and the Word of hope that's written on our hearts.

I pray for myself and all of us that God will fill us with His strength and keep our eyes fixed on Him. That He points us always in the direction that leads to our ordained path. And, that He would help us finish each day well, starting with today and finishing with the grand sum of a life well lived for Him and those we love. Oh, God of heaven, may it be!

ACKNOWLEDGEMENTS

To my wife Diana, for being the first to review and edit the chapters of this book. Thank you also for being the first to listen to every song I have ever written. I am grateful for your honesty and encouragement to finish the good stuff and leave the rest behind.

To our daughters, Niki and Nina and our Grandchildren, Luke and Eva, I am so proud of you and celebrate who you have become and are becoming. You bring joy in so many ways to our family and as we read in 3 John 1:4 "I have no greater joy than to hear that my children walk in truth."

To our family, Christy & Larry, Nick, Tracy, Maxx, Ashley & Nico, Luanne & Sky, Joanne, Carmen, Christian, Catherine & Nate, Felice, Larry, Diana, Sean, Devon & Maddy, Nick, Terra & Nicky, Linda, Al & Mia, Jeff, Joanne, David & Jan, Mary Ann, Steve & Family. Thank you for being part of our story with a lifetime of memories and so many more to come.

To Holt Vaughn, for the gift of friendship and giving your time, encouragement and expertise in the second and final editing of this book. You tirelessly poured your heart into this. You are a man of many talents and I am honored that you have shared some with me. Love also to Marietta, Evan & Jessie, & Hannah.

To Bruce Adolph and Matt Kees from Christian Musician Magazine and Christian Musician Summit, Thank you for your friendship and giving me a platform to share what God has given me for many wonderful years.

To Victor & Susan Sansone, Vito & Jeanette Iudice, Tommy & Suzie Rozzano, Richie & Phyllis Riccelli. Such a long and wonderful history together and wonderful stories not everyone will remember...but we do.

To our Canadian Family, Tore, Julie, Mercedes and Trinity Stautland, for years of friendship, encouragement & love.

To Matt Dolan for cover & graphic design. You nail it every time.

To Nikki Hollis for back cover photo. Thank you for the amazing work you do.

To Lisa Parnell for interior design and typesetting. So grateful you came on-board, I appreciate it more than you know.

To Joe Battaglia, Wes Yoder, Dr. Kevin Leman, Lynn McCain, Lannie Cates, Wayne Hastings, Lisa Murray and Laura Minchew for wise counsel and encouragement related to this book and more.

To my musician friends everywhere and especially my band mates including: Tony Hooper, Tom Lane, Will McFarlane, Anthony Morra, Emedin Rivera, Chris Taylor, Tom Rozzano, Ricky Chisholm, Ron DeRollo, Dave Hanlon, Howie Bartolo, Larry Serafini, Bob Halligan Jr., Dave Perkins, Doug Hall, Phil Keaggy, Lynn Nichols, Mike Radovsky, Mark Prentice, Robert White Johnson, Mark Doyle, Mark Pogue, Billy McDermott, Chad Welling, Rob Spagnoletti, Ronnie Leigh, Jock Guthrie, Peter York, Richard Souther, Dave Spurr, Phil Madeira, Mike Mead, Mike Caputy, Freddie Salem, David Dix, Mike Duke, Barry Graul, Russ Long, Donnie Martell, Dave Shirley, Ron Wray, Nick Caplan, Dave Frisina, Pat DeSalvo, Ronnie France, David Rezak, and from Heaven: Larry Arlotta, Matt Greeley, Duane Walker, Hughie Thomasson, Billy Jones & Dave Corcoran.

To Anadara, Charity Von, and Elias Dummer: God has given you gifts and talent in big doses. Keep using it all for Him.

The Grace Chapel Worship Team including Pastor Jonathan Allen, Tony Bostic, Debi Selby, Faith Eckland, Choir Director Kandi McIntyre, Janice Gaines, Calvin Nowell, Nicole C. Mullen, Brad Owens, Andy Cole, ALL musicians, vocalists and tech crew, including, Brant Rohwer, Joey Turner, Matt Bennett, Jon Bowen, Anita Daneker, Matt Perkins, Josh Montes, Jonathan Cox & all of our faithful volunteers. What an absolute joy lighting it up for Jesus year after year. Love Worshiping Together, Love You All!

To the Pastoral Care staff at Grace Chapel, Pastor Ron Gonser, Diana Cua, Jessie Berryman and our friends

Lyndie Gallagher, Lisa Murray, Dr. Pam Kaufman, Kamie Hefner and Patti Tremblay, thanks for loving God and people so well. Such a joy to do this together.

To the Grace Chapel Staff: Pastors Steve Berger, Mark Bright, Rob Rogers, Jonathan Allen, Jimmy Harris, Myron Goodwin, Jay Tremblay, Ian Gilchrist, David Green, Shane Eckland, Ron Clonts, Jake Spencer, Brian Ray and Dave Buehring. Sarah Berger, Donna Boone, Patrick Berger, Brooke Sawyer, Derek Brown, Katie Green, Allison Allen, Alena Dean, Nate Dickson, Tara Astafan, Adrian Riney, Bill Woodward, Rachel Bradley, Dylan & Megan Dawkins, Nick Laredo, Heather Owens, Elise Glasser, Allie Davis, Hannah Birdwell, Nicole Patterson, Catie Simpkins, Mark Supalla, Christy Haines, Gwen Mayes, Danny O'Rourke, Mike Harris, Zach Fulkerson, Ethan Henderson, Will & Jessica Miller, Michael Gallagher, Janine Harris, Jordan Birdwell, Teagan Wilkerson, Bailee Ghee, & Tahliah Peek. Thank you ALL for the love, joy and encouragement you have brought to my life.

To the staff at Kingdom Bound Ministries, Donna Russo, Wendy Menter, Amber Wing, Dave Bruno, Danielle Rose plus Lou & Liz Flis and Matt Gould and including our wonderful Volunteers & Board. Also, Pastor Dick & Mary Ann Murphy, Garry & Veronica Warden, Mike & Julia Peace, All The KB Trailer Peeps, Pastors Tommy Reid, Sam Ciffa & Samme Palermo, Steve & Charmain Tybor, Bruce & Linda Cox, Bruce Swyers, Denny Keitzman, Greg Glovins, Neil Boron, Nikki Woodford, Jody Green, Ken Loschiavo, Anthony & Chris Hoisington, Mike Failla, Alan Dusel, Jim

Orefice and Mike & Sue Gance. Thank you for over three decades of dedication to The Gospel Through The Arts.

To Tom Emmi for including me in "Lest We Forget" as we honor the great artists and musicians who have gone before us with each passing year.

To my friends, in all walks of life. I am blessed beyond measure to know you and get to do life with you. Whether a lifetime friendship or an occasional connection thank you for sharing a piece of who you are with me.

The Ministries of: Josiah's House, Giovanna's House, Randy & Amanda at Celebrate Recovery, Revive, Keith Bordeaux and Compassion International, Eight Days of Hope, Narrow Gate, A.C.T., Music Works International, The Teacher's Desk, Mercy Multiplied, Hope Clinic for Women, the efforts of Denny & Maureen Hurst and John & Janie Birdwell, Our Thrift Store, Tucker's House, One Generation Away, and Kanakuk Kamps. Caring for people the way you do has inspired me for years and helped me focus more on the needs and growth of others.

And mostly to My Lord and Savior Jesus Christ, thank you for giving me the great privilege of passing along the hope of Your Gospel through music and the spoken and written word. My greatest desire is that my life would be a strong reflection of You. "But as for me and my house we will serve the Lord." Joshua 24:15

And this important note: Surely before this ink had dried I remembered a bunch of you that I forgot to mention. Please know that I love you and I'm probably still losing sleep over it (-:

OTHER MEDIA FROM RICK

RECORDINGS:

Koo-Ah'   Within Reach
No Mystery   The Way Love Is
You're My Road   Songs To Live By
Wear Your Colors   Times Ten
Can't Stand Too Tall   Like A Cool Drink
Midnight Sun   Won't Fade Away

w/ Blues Counsel:

Let The Healing Begin   Muscle Shoals Sessions
Live At The Ramp with   Slow Demolition
Phil Keaggy   Love Infusion

w/ CRAC:
All For You

OTHER BOOK
Songs To Live By

You may contact Rick directly at
rick@rickcua.com